SECOND MARRIAGE

SECOND MARRIAGE

The Promise and the Challenge

Darlene McRoberts

AUGSBURG Publishing House
Minneapolis, Minnesota

MANUFACTURED IN THE UNITED STATES OF AMERICA

SECOND MARRIAGE

6 9/99

To Marv
whom "we" married
and whom "we" all love

Foreword

Human relationships are tested on many fronts, especially in marriage, divorce, or death of a spouse. But perhaps the area most neglected by the church and yet which carries with it many tension points is remarriage after divorce.

The silence of the church on the subject for the most part is due to continual recycling of the issue through theological or scriptural grounds (or both). Unfortunately, while the church fathers analyze and reanalyze the right or wrong of it, the people who have embarked on this uncertain journey are too often left to fend for themselves, unable to find a sympathetic ear or an understanding heart to help them rebuild.

Granted that perhaps the issue is clouded in controversy and uncertainty in the biblical sense, still people go on to try again. Every year hundreds, if not thousands, of people put aside one broken marriage relationship to try to make another work. Men and women hunger for human intimacy, love, family, and a sense of continuity in a world that is filled with lonely people. Despite the failure of one marriage pact, these people push on, hoping to make a new relationship work, to provide fathers or mothers for their children, to find for themselves the love they lost with someone else along the way. Dogma does not change that and probably never will.

With this background in mind, Darlene McRoberts has managed to articulate the issue with the same narrative power that characterized her first book, *The Hurt and Healing of Divorce*. Here, in her second book, inner fears about second marriage are clearly and sympathetically drawn with an honesty that is refreshing. The author graphically portrays both her five-year journey of going it alone after divorce and the experiences of the new relationship with humor and tears. Always frank and willing to open her heart and mind regarding a transaction still viewed as dubious by too many Christians, the author provides tremendous help and encouragement for those committed to "trying it the second time around."

This is no top-of-the-head recipe to guarantee a smooth second marriage, however. This is no quick shot at a rationale for a second marriage, either, nor is it a first aid kit to be used by those who want a quick Band-Aid to apply on the bruised mind and emotions that some second marriages bring. The author recreates in accurate detail the tension points, the fears, even the mistakes involved in rebuilding her life with another partner. In doing so she communicates something of inestimable value to those many, many souls who desperately need someone to tell them they are not alone and that their journey can be a good one, even as hers is.

Darlene McRoberts writes with a great sense of human compassion, out of experiences she has lived herself. This, coupled with her own sensitivity to Christ, the church, and biblical injunctions, gives her writing a sense of depth, maturity, and responsibility. She begins where people are, however, even as Christ himself did, and her insights take on a sense of validity and truth. It is the rare writer who can accomplish all of this with such dexterity and skill.

JAMES L. JOHNSON

Author's Acknowledgments

The subjects of second marriage and stepparent-hood are varied and complicated. My own experience demonstrates only a very small portion of the complexity of the situation. In order to present the viewpoints and experiences of many others who have also embarked on second marriage, Marv and I interviewed a number of couples, and I also interviewed some individuals. We are grateful for the time and advice the following people gave so freely and willingly, contributing much to the value and authenticity of this book: Dr. Kenneth D. Barringer, Dr. Wesley L. Brun, Jack and Marilyn Cushman, Douglas and Hellen Dawson, Dr. Walter Johnson, Marianne Kwiecinski, Michael Henry Martin, Ferdinand and Florence Pauls, Ray and Joy Strutz, and Loni Whitfield.

Also, special thanks to my pastor, Ken Stangeland, and my good friend, Sandra Tymoszenko, for their professional input.

I also want to express my thanks to those who prefer to remain nameless, as well as to those authors whose work is quoted in this book, and to their publishers, who gave us reprint permission.

Lastly, I want to again thank my husband, who spent long, tedious hours transcribing the many taped interviews, and my kids, for understanding when I had to say, "I can't play now. I've got to work on my book." They were great.

Throughout the book, I refer to the situation of marrying again to a new person as remarriage, or second marriage. The term remarriage also applies to people who divorce and then remarry the same person, of course, but in the context of this book, we are discussing people who remarried a new spouse. There were, also, a few instances where someone we interviewed happened to be in a third marriage (as there possibly will be readers in the third marriages), but I do not believe this alters the information being discussed.

DARLENE McROBERTS
Elmhurst, Illinois
September, 1977

Introduction

The five members of our family were preparing to sit down to Sunday breakfast—all the while carrying on a colorful discussion as to who takes the longest to get dressed on weekday mornings.

As a preface to some point she never got around to making, my 17-year-old daughter Pam said to my husband, "Before we married you last June . . . ."

"Say," I interrupted, "what do you mean, before *we* married Marv last June? I was under the impression that *I* was the one who married him."

"Well, now, I don't know about that," Marv grinned. "Seems to me I sort of inherited the whole bunch of you. Sort of a package deal, wouldn't you say?"

"And see how lucky you were," Pam teased back, as her two younger brothers shook their heads and grinned.

Later, Marv and I talked more about Pam's casual comment. We decided it was an affirmation of our marriage, showing that the kids recognized they were a real part of our marriage. *We had become a family.*

This had been one of our goals all along. We had hoped it would work out that way—but it hadn't happened overnight and the adjustments hadn't been easy.

CHAPTER ONE

The Dating Game

One day Jan, my associate editor, casually mentioned that she and her husband, Vern, had been talking about introducing me to one of Vern's co-workers. I was hesitant. I could picture coming to work and having to tell her that I was not impressed by her matchmaking, which might hurt our comfortable friendship.

On the other hand, I did like what she told me about this man. They had decided to tell each of us only a little about the other, allowing us to arrive at our own conclusions.

Cleverly, they asked Marv and me to their home to watch a Chicago-Green Bay football game. I planned to arrive early and change from my work clothes to more comfortable slacks and a sweater. However, I was delayed. Sure enough, when I pulled up, an unfamiliar car was already parked in front of their house.

Ringing the bell took every ounce of my courage. Marv was sitting right inside the door. And there I stood, slacks and sweater rolled in a ball in my arms, trying to look composed, as though I had blind dates all the time.

The evening was fantastic. After the game, we all sat on the floor, talking and laughing. Marv and I leaned against the couch, pushing a football back and forth while we talked, feeling as though we had known each other forever. We probably could have talked all night, but our host and hostess looked as if they were getting sorrier by the minute that they had invited two people who didn't seem to know when to go home. It was also obvious that they intended for us to leave together.

Marv walked me to my car, said goodnight—and did not ask for my phone number. As I drove home, I thought about this neat guy. But I warned myself about taking him too seriously—we were obviously different in many ways.

He had mentioned his fondness for catfish. Egads! I thought of catfish as scavengers, a catch not worth bragging about, much less eating. And he swam in the Mississippi River. I love to swim in clear Wisconsin lakes—but the Mississippi River? Obviously, I thought, our likings are very different and nothing will ever come of this matchmaking.

The next morning at work, I felt none of the awkwardness I had feared. Having had a great time, I couldn't wait to thank Jan. She seemed disappointed, however, when I admitted that Marv hadn't asked for my phone number. She evidently concluded that I hadn't made much of an impression.

Tuesday night I stayed home and worked on a book I was writing. Every time the phone rang, I thought, "Could it be Marv?" Yet I knew it couldn't be, because my phone number was unlisted.

The next morning Jan had good news. "Guess who stopped by the house last night *for your phone number*," she teased.

Marv called that night, before I was prepared. I had envisioned answering the phone in a casual, slightly sexy tone of voice. But he called just when I was trying to get supper on the table. All three children were sitting between me and the phone. Although the cord was long enough to reach the stove, I ended up burning the meat. (I never have been good at doing two things at once.) The kids' voices came through over the phone loud and clear. I could hear dimes being deposited, so I realized Marv was calling from a phone booth and this was costing him plenty.

He invited me out for Sunday brunch. I didn't know what to say. While I was free Friday night and Saturday night, Sunday after church I was invited for dinner to the home of Bob and Alyce Stoeck, a couple who had been my friends for years. But I accepted his invitation and decided I'd figure out later how to be two places at once.

The next day was my turn to ask Jan for Marv's phone number. I called Bob and Alyce and asked if I could bring a friend along to dinner. They sound-ed a bit skeptical when I told them I had only met Marv two days earlier, but they graciously agreed. Then I worked up enough nerve to call Marv. He agreed to the new plans right away—and invited himself over that very night.

Again I panicked. My house was a disaster! The kids and I had moved in only a month earlier, and since I had a book deadline pressing, I had left all the non-urgent boxes right where we'd put them the day we moved, in the middle of the dining room.

Marv arrived (early, of course) at the front door, which was blocked by a couch. I had to dash around from the back door to invite him to come to the rear.

Marv had given some serious thought to his initial impression on my kids, and had decided to resort to "bribery," as he put it. His first few visits especially endeared him to my boys because he brought potato chips, soft drinks, and fruit along for treats.

Marv later told me that he had learned the value of bribery from his own stepfather, Connie, who had used the same technique on Marv and his sisters while courting Vala, Marv's mother. It obviously had worked, because Marv has remembered it all those years.

The first evening Marv came to visit worked out well, considering. There were a few rough spots. My sons decided to bring out scads of old snapshots, including some with their father's picture. I don't know whether this was deliberate, but I felt uncomfortable, to say the least.

However, I appreciated Marv's willingness to let the children get acquainted with him before we actually dated. This was especially important to me since I had made a few bad moves when I first resumed dating, which had been threatening to my sons. Once or twice, I had left my young sons with their older sister while I went out with a man whom the kids had just met. They were terrified that this stranger was "taking me away from them." This is a common experience of kids who have recently "lost" one parent from their home. They fear this stranger will take away their remaining parent, too.

After a couple of teary-eyed, almost hysterical good-byes, I had decided this wasn't worth it. Then I made a second bad move. I decided it would be better to meet my date at the nearest shopping center. But I wasn't fooling the kids. This only made them even more insecure and afraid to trust me. So, by the time I met Marv, I had made up my mind never to go out with anyone until my boys had an opportunity to become acquainted with him. I'd invite the fellow over to spend some time just talking and watching television, attempting to reassure the boys he wasn't going to whisk me away from them. (Had any man refused, I would have realized our relationship wasn't worth continuing.)

Marv knew about these past problems and was especially understanding. In fact, he was often the one who insisted we include the children in our plans. So a date for Marv and me often meant Saturday night with the boys at the ice skating rink or a Walt Disney movie. (Pam, by then, usually had her own plans.)

As a result, the children didn't feel as fearful toward Marv as they had toward some of my earlier dates. But I sometimes found the arrangements frustrating. It was difficult, if not impossible, to appear especially charming or "feminine" while racing across the ice with my sons and occasionally falling flat on my face. It was equally difficult to appear serene and poised while scolding a six-year-old for spilling popcorn on the head of the woman sitting in front of him.

First-timers have a luxury not available to second-timers with children: *time alone.* This was a very valuable commodity for us. When we made an effort to have time to ourselves, usually we had to pay a babysitter, and we often phoned home to be sure everything was okay.

We tried to arrange our evenings together so we could spend time with the children and then, after the children went to bed, have time to ourselves. But it wasn't as easy as it sounds. For one thing, Marv has to get up each morning at 5:00 A.M., so he retires early. Also, though the boys seemed somewhat relaxed when they were included in our activities, they still felt threatened when Marv stayed around after they were in bed. I didn't want to increase this fear, so one night early in our dating days when Tim came wandering downstairs half-asleep, I let him lie on the couch next to me, hoping he would drift back to sleep. I thought this might convince him that he wasn't missing anything and had nothing to worry about. But he was determined not to sleep and started snapping bubble gum to help himself stay awake. Consequently, my conversation with

Marv was accentuated by a nerve-wracking cracking of gum, and we were both ready to climb the wall. I was concerned that Tim's feelings would intensify if I sent him back to bed, but I also worried that Marv would be irritated.

Neither Tim's younger brother or older sister exhibited such a strong reaction to Marv. But Tim seemed convinced that I couldn't love both Marv and him. As he became aware that my affection for Marv was increasing, he assumed I was loving him less. No matter how many times I tried to convince him that I would always love him and that my love for him had nothing to do with my affection toward Marv, he couldn't seem to grasp this. Marv tried to explain to Timmy that he was beginning to love him too, so there was now an extra person who loved him; he had much to gain and nothing to lose. But Tim's intense anxiety didn't disappear easily.

It soon showed up again. On one of his early visits to our home, Marv walked in the door and practically threw a brown bag into my arms, with a shy "Here." In it were four lovely roses, three yellow and one red. Marv explained these represented my three kids and me. I was thrilled and touched.

Timmy, however, felt threatened by Marv's gift to me. A few days later, he spent all his money on a huge, beautiful plant, which he eagerly carried home. Unfortunately, I was on the phone talking to Marv when Tim arrived to present it to me. Even though I made a big deal over it, I could see my being on the phone with "that man" just at the moment of his special presentation took the edge off his pleasure.

Marv and I talked about the turmoil my kids were in. Although he didn't always agree with my approach, he was concerned that he not become any more of a threat to them. His sensitivity to the problem made me care for him even more.

After we'd been dating a few weeks, Marv mentioned that we had been extremely fortunate in the manner in which we met. Our friends had made it much more pleasant for us than if we had had to go out alone on a blind date. Their home provided a familiar common ground for us. I felt the same way.

From the very beginning Marv and I were comfortable with each other, as though we had known each other a long time. When we went to my friends' home for dinner the very first Sunday after we met, we already felt at ease together. Of course, it helped that Bob and Alyce went out of their way to create a relaxed atmosphere, and we had a wonderful day. On our way back to my house that evening, we both commented that we could hardly believe we had only known each other six days. We felt like we'd been friends for years.

I found that I could tell a lot about a man by his willingness to establish relationships with my friends. Does he care enough to become acquainted, and is he willing to bend a bit, knowing how important this is to me? I felt that any man I would consider marrying would have to enjoy the friends that meant the most to me. I would not allow friends' reactions to dictate whether I continued seeing someone, but I believed that if a potential husband didn't relate well to most of my friends, this would eventually become a major problem in our relationship. Some marriages have deteriorated primarily because one partner had to give up friends their spouse didn't enjoy. I believe this is especially important in second marriages because usually in the former marriages the individuals had a number of years to establish close friendships, and they do not want to break ties with these friends just because their marriage has dissolved.

Although Marv and I felt comfortable together and I appreciated so much his efforts to make my friends his friends, I realized that we were two very different people. I worried whether we could adapt to each other's life-styles and interests. I tried to tell myself that it was much too early in our relationship to even give this serious thought. But if we *were* incompatible, I thought too much of Marv to allow us to begin to care too much for each other. I decided we should nip this romance in the bud before we ended up hurting each other. (Marv was going through similar mental gymnastics.) However, while my mind was telling me to be sensible and cautious, I found myself increasingly drawn to this man.

"Don't ever ask me to go to church with you," he said determinedly one day. "As far as I can see, most people who are busy going to church all the time are hypocrites—at least that has sometimes been my experience."

So I didn't ask him to go to church with me. Then one Sunday afternoon when he came over after I had returned from church, he asked, "How come you never invite me to go to church with you?" The next Sunday he picked up the kids and me and we all went to church together. And he liked it very much—he liked our pastor and our congregation, even the sermon and most of the music.

Just a few weeks later, Corrie ten Boom was scheduled to speak at a huge church nearby. I had read her book, *The Hiding Place,* and eagerly planned to attend. Since Marv usually spent all day Sunday with us, I went ahead and made plans with two other couples to meet us there . . . and then held my breath as I cautiously mentioned the subject to Marv. Although he didn't seem particularly thrilled, he agreed to go.

We left the house fairly early, but when we arrived at the church parking lot we couldn't believe the crowds. Many were even leaving because there was such an overflow. But I was so eager to hear her and to have Marv hear her that I talked Marv into at least trying to find a spot for us to park. Amazingly, in spite of the huge crowd (many were sitting in overflow rooms where they could hear but not see Corrie), somehow we ended up with two good seats. I believe this was a special blessing from God. When he wants us to get a particular message, he works things out just right.

Marv was as delighted with Corrie as I was. We both will always remember one lesson she taught us that night. She quoted from the Bible: "As far as the east is from the west, so far hath he removed our transgressions from us" (Ps. 103:12). And she added, "Then God puts up a No Fishing sign."

I believe that example of God's love and forgiveness was something Marv and I both needed to hear; and especially Marv, since he did not have the support of a forgiving, loving Christian community, as I did.

Whenever a person is involved in a divorce, whether that person initiated it, amicably agreed to it, or was an unwilling participant, there are almost always deep accompanying feelings of guilt. In some cases, these may be just occasional pangs, usually at a lonely moment. But in most instances, the feelings are painful and depressing.

Marv's divorce had not been caused by any dramatic problem—certainly not involvement with a third party. And Marv had been extremely generous in the financial settlement. He had little reason to suffer from extreme guilt feelings—but he did. To make his feelings even more intense, his former wife became ill after their divorce and he was left feeling somehow responsible, although from a medical standpoint that was very improbable. He again contributed much financial support, but he found that paying house payments and hospital bills couldn't erase his guilt feelings.

Unfortunately, many divorced people carry these feelings right into a new marriage. Since the guilt feelings do not disappear without being adequately faced and dealt with, they often end up contaminating the new relationship. It is like buying a brand new home and decorating it, but failing to get rid of that bag of stinky garbage left under the sink. That one little bag of garbage can smell up the entire house.

I believe that when a marriage falls apart, it is usually the result of two people's mistakes. Frequently people marry without really knowing each other— or maybe not really knowing themselves. As years progress they mature and discover how different they really are. Some such marriages, in the words of the popular *Ladies' Home Journal* feature, can "be saved." But sometimes things get continually worse and the children become meshed in this emotional mixup. Too many people today merely "tolerate" their marriages.

As I pointed out in my book, *The Hurt and Healing of Divorce*, statistics indicate that children caught in intolerable home situations are much worse off than children whose parents get a clean-cut divorce. I also believe that there are couples who, although they try very hard, pray about their marriage, and even seek counseling, simply find living together impossible. And, though it certainly is not God's perfect will, I believe he is willing to forgive the couple and set them free to live apart.

Happily, many times when two people really commit their marriage to the Lord and seek professional guidance, things do improve and gradually they find they can make their marriage work, but in other cases all signs point to separation. Then it is time to stop pretending and start new separate lives. Couples do not do each other a favor by sticking with a bad marriage to prevent hurting each other. The other is already hurting from the inadequate relationship. God has put such a high value on human beings, I do not believe he forces us to suffer a whole lifetime for a mistake made while young and emotional, or, for that matter, for mistakes made later in life.

Corrie ten Boom's vivid description of how complete God's forgiving power is, made an indelible impression on both Marv and me. Later that evening we talked about God's love and forgiveness. I asked Marv if he wanted us to pray together and we did, for the first time. We asked God to rid us of our feelings of guilt and we received his forgiveness for our many mistakes. I believe he gave Marv and me a special blessing that evening.

Since Marv had been very enthusiastic about Corrie ten Boom, the very next day I went on my lunch hour to buy *The Hiding Place* for him. I'd found it a difficult book to get into, so I realized Marv might lose interest. My worry was needless; he'd read the entire book by the next time I saw him, and we talked about it at length. He liked it so much, he even recommended it to others.

Thus started my secret plan to start Marv on a reading program. I wanted to introduce him to interesting Christian books and personalities, taking care not to bore him or overwhelm him. I knew he would love Jim Johnson's Sebastian novels, so I gave him the first in the series. He enjoyed it and was anxious to start the next one. Now he often reminds me that the next time I talk to Jim on the phone at work, I should be sure to tell him to get busy writing more Sebastian books, since his fans are waiting.

I continued my little plan, passing books, magazines, and clippings on to Marv. I was very selective about church activities I invited him to attend. I wanted to be sure I didn't turn him off in my eagerness to help him get to know Jesus better.

I never pressed him or even asked him to join my church, but less than six months after our marriage, he announced that he would like to join. I was delighted. We attended a weekly membership class together. I found this was a good review and renewal for me, and especially meaningful to share with Marv.

Then, early in December of 1975, Marv was accepted as a member of Grace Lutheran Church. Because of my close ties with this congregation, I was especially thrilled.

Since my divorce, I had tried to stretch my income to support three kids and myself by doing free-lance writing in addition to my daytime job as an editor. When I met Marv, I was already knee-deep in writing my book about divorce. Since then, I have worried that the book might have suffered, because my mind was soon more on love than divorce; by the time I completed that book, Marv and I were talking about getting married.

Marv was especially considerate of the large amount of time which I needed to spend glued to my typewriter. In fact, he helped to keep the kids occupied and even picked up hamburgers and fries for us on many Sunday evenings while I worked on the book.

Although it hasn't been easy for him, Marv has adjusted quite nicely to the deadline dilemmas I face. As much as his organized mind can bear, he allows things to pile up "until the book is done." I completed three books during the first 30 months I knew Marv, so he was rapidly introduced to what working against deadlines is like. In fact, our very first argument was about a deadline—on my birthday, no less.

Marv came over the evening of my birthday (the first since we'd met). He brought me a mother's bracelet, which I loved. Then, after we had filled up on goodies, I told him that I had an article which had to be finished by the next morning. Before he left, I was typing away madly. He came over to my desk to kiss me goodbye. That was fine, of course. But he also had a few things to say. Shaking his finger at me in a parental way, he proclaimed emphatically, "You are not going to do this anymore."

Although he had good intentions, this hit me hard as a reprimand which I didn't feel I deserved. Actually, to use transactional analysis jargon, I felt that what I really deserved was a "warm fuzzy." At the very least, I was hoping for a word of encouragement: "You can do it!" But I felt no support in his tone of voice or his pointing finger.

To make a long story short, I overreacted and Marv scolded some more and we wasted a great deal of precious time. After we finally made up and he left, my eyes stung from crying and I still had that article to complete by the next day.

We've talked about that argument since then—in fact, I've brought it up a few times too many. Now I realize it wasn't so much *what* Marv was saying— he had my health in mind. It was a matter of semantics—*how* he said it. I heard in him an angry parent scolding me and I reacted as a frustrated child.

We have had similar disagreements stemming from Marv's tendency to parent me and my defensive reaction to that behavior. Now we recognize what is happening. But there are still times. . . .

Regarding my writing assignments, however, Marv has become much more patient. Occasionally he doesn't realize the deep concentration I need to "get into" the subject after being away from my desk a while. He'll say, "Come here a minute, dear" for some little thing which could have waited, just when my mind is beginning to click. But if your husband is making supper and it smells delicious, should you complain if he interrupts to ask what kind of vegetable you'd prefer?

After Marv and I had been dating for a while and we began to realize how much we cared for each other, I wondered whether he had told his parents about me. I was especially concerned because of my three children. I had dated one man whose mother was very upset that he was seeing a divorced woman with three kids.

One evening Marv said, "Well, I called Mother today." I held my breath. "Did you mention us?" I hesitantly asked.

"Why, sure," Marv grinned. "At first she asked if I knew what I was getting into. Of course, I reminded her that Connie had gotten into the same situation." (Connie is Marv's stepfather. Marv's mother had been widowed with three children.) "And after that she was just fine. In fact, she wants to know when I am going to bring you all down to meet her."

I sighed in relief, although I knew that the real test was yet to come—when she was actually with the kids.

We decided that Marv would take me down to meet his family first, while the kids were in Wisconsin with their natural dad for Christmas vacation.

Marv grew up in Port Byron, Illinois, on the Mississippi River, and his parents still live there. We set out to drive down the Sunday after Christmas—a lovely, crisp snowy day. We talked all the way, trying to hide that little bit of nervousness we were both experiencing. Both of us wanted everything to go smoothly.

I followed Marv's example and brought along a little bribe—just a small hanging plant for his mom, but one picked with lots of hope and anticipation.

Vala, Marv's mom, walked out to the car, and I liked her immediately. The day was great. I met Marv's entire family—his sisters and their husbands and children. I admired Connie. He, like everyone else, went out of his way to welcome me. Marv and I sang all the way home.

However, the day was still ahead when we would bring the kids to be "checked out." Once we set a date to get married, we felt this should be next on our priority list. We decided Danny's birthday would be a good time. We planned to bring a birthday cake along, but Vala wouldn't hear of it. She baked one for him herself.

In the car I gave the kids thousands of orders all the way there. And, of course, they immediately forgot most of them. But Vala and Connie and the others were fantastic. My kids loved having all these new cousins and relatives.

There were a few bad moments. The kids talked back to Marv once in front of his family, and of course that was the last thing I wanted to happen. Both Marv and I were so anxious to do everything right that we had splitting headaches and made nervous wrecks out of ourselves and each other. But we left with a sense of relief—I felt accepted and realized they were welcoming the kids with open arms. It was even better than I had hoped.

It took a while before I could relax with the kids in front of Marv's folks. I was very conscious of everything they said and did and I probably made everyone uncomfortable. But now I feel at home with them and I think they feel the same about me.

Marv's folks have a fantastic houseboat which Connie built with Vala's help. Our kids love being on it, and so do we. That was a bonus. We have all learned to love the river. I can't believe I once thought I'd never swim in it. We swim, boat, relax, and fish in it with great pleasure.

My parents invited Marv and me out to dinner shortly after I started dating Marv. They liked him and felt he would be good for me and the kids. However, since Marv wasn't bringing any new grandchildren into their lives, they didn't have the "opportunity" Marv's family did to welcome an entire brood.

CHAPTER TWO

The Wedding

As time went on, while we frequently warned each other not to become too serious in our relationship, deep down we both realized that we already were serious. Our conversations began to include such phrases as "next year." Then began the "if we should happen to decide to get married someday" comments.

One night, Marv and I were sitting on the couch, talking and cuddling, and he asked me, "Are you going to marry me?" It came out so unexpectedly that, after only a moment's hesitation, I rather flippantly replied, "Well, yes, someday." Then he got more specific and asked, "When?" and I knew he was serious.

I thought about it for a while and realized that I was unexpectedly committing myself sooner than I had anticipated—yet I didn't ask that we table the question for a while.

After a few moments, I said, "Well, I don't know. Why not plan to get married next year (this was March of '75) and make it our bicentennial thing?"

He said he didn't see why we should wait that long, but he didn't push it any further. The conversation was very matter-of-fact and we did not discuss it any more that evening.

After Marv left, what had transpired between us really sank in. Why, we had agreed we would get married! I felt a slight hesitation. All those years in a first marriage that didn't work out had impressed on me the importance of not rushing into another relationship. And here I had just committed myself to a new marriage, so easily and quickly. Marv later told me that he had thought somewhat the same thing on his way home. He had asked himself, "Are you sure you know what you're getting into?" Actually, he would be taking a more drastic step than I, since he would be taking on a whole family.

It wasn't long before Marv began teasing me about waiting until the bicentennial year. I would tease back, "If it's for real, it will keep." But as we mentioned things like camping next summer, we began to realize that neither of us particularly wanted to go camping in separate trailers or without each other.

Soon he brought it up in a serious conversation. He pointed out that we were practically supporting the local gas station and telephone company with our calls and trips back and forth. Besides, saying goodnight was getting more and more difficult, and sleeping alone had suddenly become very lonely.

We decided to get married that June. As soon as we decided, we called a meeting with my kids and told them about our plans. Pam was delighted and Dan also seemed happy. Even Tim, to our surprise, seemed to accept the news quite well. We promised that they would be involved in our wedding service. When they mentioned accompanying us on a honeymoon weekend, however, we drew the line.

We had to compromise about what kind of a wedding to have. Marv's first inclination was to simply ask our pastor to marry us with little fanfare. But I wanted some of our friends to celebrate this happy occasion with us. I also wanted to take some of those friends out for a nice meal, since they had been supportive to me during my divorced years. We soon found out that restaurant reservations should have been made months earlier, and we almost gave up. But then we remembered a delightful restaurant that had not only delicious food but also a beautiful farmlike atmosphere. They had one date left open in June. We grabbed it.

We were almost afraid to phone our pastor to ask if he and the church were available that June afternoon. But things worked out just fine.

We started making up a guest list. We especially wanted to invite those friends who had been closest to us during the difficult time while we were each divorced. But soon we realized we couldn't possibly afford to invite all our friends. Eventually we decided only to invite friends that both of us had become close to as a couple.

We decided we wanted our invitation worded: "Please join us in celebrating our marriage, on Sunday, June 22, 1975, at 2:30 o'clock in the afternoon." Then we selected an antique beige paper with a simple gold cross. Soon the invitations were on their way.

A trip to the library failed to produce any information or ideas on etiquette for second weddings, so we felt perfectly free to do things just the way we wanted. I knew I would feel uncomfortable walking down the aisle with Marv waiting for me at the altar. We decided to simply walk in together just before the service and sit in the front pew.

The most difficult decision was who to ask to stand up for us. But since we wanted to be sure the children felt included, we decided to ask Pam to be my attendant and have the two boys stand at Marv's side, each holding a wedding band.

Since we also wanted to include some of our friends, we decided to ask three special couples to each participate in the early part of the service. Before the actual ceremony, each couple would give a short, informal talk about love and marriage.

Since we were planning an informal wedding, we decided to invite the guests to join in singing, so we had bulletins made up with the words to "Pass It On," "Bless This Day, Bless Our Friends" (adapted to the tune of "Edelweiss"), and "Blest Be the Tie That Binds." Pam was to accompany the singing with her guitar and our friend Karen Long added the piano background. Marv's niece and nephew and our two boys would stand up in front of the church and lead the guests in singing. After the ceremony, Karen would scoot over to the organ and we would recess to the singing of "Blest Be the Tie." We were very happy with this selection; all the songs had special meaning to us.

June 22 dawned as the hottest day of the year, if not the century. Marv insisted on ignoring the old adage about the groom not seeing the bride before the wedding. He came over to drive us to the church. I think he wanted to check us over ahead of time, to see if we all met with his approval. On the way to the church, he decided to stop at a department store and buy Tim a different pair of socks. He was unhappy with the tube socks Tim was wearing.

We had fun greeting our guests—one of the advantages of second weddings. Then it was time for the service to begin.

Marv and I waited at the back of the church for Timmy to light the candles—our signal to walk to the first pew. Then our pastor's son came running up the back stairs and said, "Hey, Timmy needs some matches." Whenever we had practiced lighting the candles, there had always been two or three matchboxes put in the back room for that purpose. Today there were none! We scrounged some up quickly, from a guest sitting nearest the back of the church.

We held our breath as Tim had a bit of trouble lighting the second candle. No one but us realized that even on his tiptoes he barely could reach the very top. Then we quietly walked to our pew, ready to enjoy the ceremony.

It was fun singing at our own wedding, and we loved the kind and clever things each of the three couples had to say. Vern and Jan told how Jan had volunteered Vern to help me move and how Vern decided, after lugging my washer and dryer upstairs and into the truck almost by himself, that I needed "someone much closer to her to whom she could turn for help the next time she decided to move. So Marvin seemed ideal."

Then they continued, "While we are good friends now, we want to make sure that we remain that way and that someday we don't get all the blame for the introduction. So we have compiled a few suggestions which we hope will keep Marvin and Darlene compatible forever—and at the same time guarantee that they will remain our friends." They had made up a beautiful little booklet titled "Rules for a Happy Marriage."

Then Bud and Judy added their special thoughts and some lovely poetry. Char and Bill emphasized the importance of allowing Christ to be the Lord of our marriage and concluded with meaningful Bible verses. Then we sang again, and Pam read 1 Corinthians 13.

Pastor asked Marv and me and the kids all to come to the altar. Marv and I partook of Holy Communion. Then, facing each other, we promised to love and cherish each other. Pastor shared some beautiful thoughts, reminding us that we had selected

40

each other from the whole world and admonished us to keep Christ as head of our home and our lives, and to pray together and read God's Word together.

After we recessed, we turned around to watch Danny extinguish the candles. But Danny was still sitting on a step at the foot of the chancel, solemnly watching the guests. Pam, with the help of her long-time friend Doug, was planning to usher out the guests *after* Danny put out the candles. She was trying unsuccessfully to get Danny's attention. We quietly walked back towards the front of the church, also motioning to him. Then suddenly he remembered and (while we held our breath) put the candles out exactly the way we had practiced.

Many friends told us they thought the service was lovely, and we agreed.

The joyous reception was a combination of feasting, celebrating, and enjoying our friends. It will always remain a precious memory to us. We have the service on tape and lots of pictures. We plan to use these every year on our anniversary to regain for a few moments those special memories.

We have always been glad that we included the children in our plans for our wedding, as well as in the wedding itself. Most second-timers with children agree.

Interestingly, Amy Vanderbilt, well-known authority on etiquette, did an about-face on this subject. In *Amy Vanderbilt's New Complete Book of Etiquette* (which we had not seen before our wedding, though it wouldn't have changed our feelings), she stated briefly:

It is poor taste for young children of the first marriage to even attend the marriage of either parent the second time, if a divorce has taken place. . . . When there is remarriage after divorce and there are children of a previous marriage old enough to understand and perhaps resent all the implications of the new marriage, it is certainly more tactful to be married without any but the necessary legal witnesses than to have a small wedding from which the children must be excluded.

But when Amy Vanderbilt celebrated her fourth marriage to divorced attorney Curtis Kellar, her three children and his five were all included in the reception. She admitted she had been very wrong. "My boys were furious at the idea of being left out," she explained.

One man went a step further. Sherry tells how, on Valentine's Day, Tom had asked her to have dinner with him. He insisted that her two daughters, ages 9 and 11, be at home when he picked her up.

When he arrived, he asked Sherry and the girls to sit on the couch. From his pocket, he took three small boxes. Two contained a heart-shaped ring with a tiny diamond in the center. The other contained a diamond engagement ring. Sherry said, "He proposed to all three of us and, needless to say, I didn't have a chance. The four of us have been married now for three and a half years" (from *Reader's Digest*, Life in These United States).

CHAPTER THREE

The Period
of Adjustment

After the wedding comes the marriage, beginning with a period of adjustment. When two divorced or widowed persons remarry in the movies, they seem to successfully blend their many children with few problems. And, of course, the problems are always hilariously funny.

But no matter how hard we tried to take ourselves lightly and laugh at our mistakes, often we became angry or frustrated or discouraged—sometimes all three at the same time.

Though from the beginning Marv and I felt comfortable with each other, at times it seemed like we were on opposite tracks—or worse yet, on the same track, coming from opposite directions at full speed.

Marv is compulsively neat. One day when I dug my grapefruit knife out of the silverware drawer I discovered it had been straightened. When questioned, Marv admitted he had seen this crooked knife and just couldn't resist straightening it out. As I tried to bend it back in shape, I explained that grapefruit knives are *supposed* to be curved.

Marv also believes that everything has a place and belongs there. Seventeen years with kids around had indoctrinated me to the premise that some things just aren't worth the hassle. I can close my eyes to shoes left astray and go happily on my way. But Marv's position was, "I'm not afraid to hassle. People should learn to put things where they belong."

Nothing went unseen by Marv. He never missed an ice cream scoop left dripping on the counter or a bar of soap left dissolving in bathwater. Sometimes I'd quietly slip out of the room, leaving him alone with the guilty party. Other times, when I realized the situation warranted my support, I stood with him.

I was delighted one day when I came across a book titled *How to Do Things Right: The Revelations of a Fussy Man* by L. Rust Hills. Not only was the book perfect for Marv—it did me a world of good to realize that Mrs. Hills had survived being married to a perfectionist.

Lillian Messinger, in a report on "Remarriage Between Divorced People with Children from Previous Marriages" *(Journal of Marriage and Family Counseling)*, says:

> There is disagreement regarding the success rate of remarriage compared to first marriages. Monahan (1959) reports that the divorce-remarried have higher rates of divorce in their second and

subsequent marriages than do first marrieds. Goode (1965) and Bernard (1971) suggest there is little difference in the divorce rates of the two groups. These discrepancies may be due to the different data bases of the studies cited. We might expect that differences in these success rates will decline over time as divorce, as a solution to marital problems, is chosen by a broader spectrum of the population.

When we were first married, I felt a tremendous responsibility to compensate or make up to Marv for the extra work and lack of privacy he had to endure because of my three children. It became a serious problem to me—a real burden. I was always remembering the spotlessly clean, quiet home he had been used to in his first marriage.

I was especially conscious of the situation after school. Marv goes to work at 5:30 A.M. and returns home at 3:30 P.M. The boys return home about the same time, which leaves Marv no time to have the house to himself, no opportunity for a bit of peace and quiet before the boys tear in. Any naps he may try to squeeze in are usually disturbed by the Mickey Mouse Club, the boys' friends at the door, and numerous other interruptions.

But this situation also gave Marv an opportunity to establish a relationship with the boys. He was usually willing to play ball, work on models, or help them with their homework. He also helps them with their chore of doing dishes.

I believe this aspect of our marriage was another answered prayer. For a long time before meeting Marv, I was concerned that the boys needed more

45

male models. I had made a point of hiring a high school boy to babysit occasionally the previous summer and I had recently made arrangements for the boys to meet regularly with a male counselor. But I still didn't feel that the boys were getting the kind of male influence they needed and I didn't know how long I would be able to afford to pay for professional help. Only a few months before meeting Marv, I prayed with a friend especially about this situation.

Maybe I was running ahead of God again—praying for an answer and at the same time trying to solve the problem my own way. I am always uncertain how much effort one should put forth when asking for God's help. Often answers to my prayers have come from the most unexpected places. Yet at other times, answers have come as a direct result of my getting out and seeking practical solutions.

In this case, God's answer was to provide Marv—a man who likes sports, who was interested in establishing a relationship with the boys, and, to make it better yet, who gets off work early enough to be home when the boys return from school.

But God doesn't always answer our prayers this quickly or this directly. Often he expects *us* to do the leg work. I especially like the saying of Martin Luther, "Work as though it all depends on you and pray as though it all depends on God."

Though we don't consider it a big problem, one other adjustment is our name, which is not the same as that of our kids. When Marv began coaching Tim's baseball team, the boys, most of whom Tim had just met, assumed that Marv's last name was the same as

Tim's so they called Marv "Mr. Petri." After a while, it got tiresome to keep correcting the kids and we learned to ignore it. Many of the parents also picked up Tim's last name and called us by that, too. Also, many of the friends our kids already had, who were used to calling me Mrs. Petri, had a terrible time getting used to calling me Mrs. McRoberts.

Since each year we seem to meet new kids, the situation recurs from time to time. A new room mother will call up and ask for Mrs. Petri. That is not quite as confusing as when a baseball manager calls up and asks for Mr. Petri. Sometimes we aren't sure, at first, that he doesn't actually mean Tim's natural father. There is nothing we can do but accept this situation and get used to it.

Another of my concerns, when Marv and I were first married, was that we might become so bogged down with day-to-day "parenting" that we would lose the special closeness we had felt while getting acquainted with each other.

One way we prevented this was by attending college together. I had started attending evening school shortly after getting divorced and had continued most of the time thereafter. After I explained to Marv that it was important for me to continue, he decided he would like to go with me. We chose a course in American history, which we continued for three quarters and thoroughly enjoyed. We had some trouble finding time to study and even more trouble finding time for the required outside reading, but somehow we did fit it all in. It gave us much to talk about together and to share with the kids.

Our first family vacation was a fall camping trip in Door County, Wisconsin. One rainy day found us cozy in our sleeping bags, rain pounding on the tarpaulin outside, but all of us engrossed in our history books inside. I thoroughly enjoyed *Those Who Love,* a biography of Abigail Adams, while Marv found a biography of Nathanael Greene interesting. The kids had plenty of their own outside reading for school to keep them occupied.

The following spring, my company sent me to the Evangelical Press Convention in Philadelphia. We decided to really do our bicentennial thing big and all go. By the time we toured Pennsylvania we were up to our ears in history.

Once we were in the habit of attending school, we weighed the advantages against the disadvantages and both agreed we should continue. We had misgivings about leaving the kids with a babysitter two nights a week, but we knew we were setting a good example for them when we all sat down to study together. Also, we were helping them see that learning should be a continuing, lifetime experience.

Besides, we knew we were putting a priority on our relationship, taking care that there was more to it than being parents. And our conversations, in the car and around the supper table, were certainly more interesting as a result of our studies.

The next year we enrolled in psychology, and we found many opportunities to share our newest bits of knowledge. The outside reading and discussions were fascinating. We've also completed classes in child development and business management.

The class that provided the most fun was probably physical education. We began with volleyball. Many of our adjustment problems seemed to come to a head on the volleyball court.

Both of us love the game, but being on the same team had its disadvantages. Marv's habit of parenting me (or his male chauvinism) became quite apparent when he continually told me what I was doing wrong, or worse yet, hogged my ball. My lack of self-confidence quickly showed up. The minute he criticized me, I'd go to pieces. And when he'd fail to notice my good moves, I'd feel sorry for myself.

It became a vicious circle. Once I felt sorry for myself or upset with Marv, I'd flub the next ball that came my way, then feel angry at myself and project that anger at Marv. It really spoiled all the fun, which made me especially exasperated with myself.

Then came the last straw. One evening I felt weak and dizzy and decided to stay home. Marv talked me into going, saying that a little fun and exercise might be just what I needed. So I went, still feeling miserable.

That night, Marv was selected as one of the captains. I breathed a sigh of relief, sure that I would be on his team. Tonight I would be delighted if he played my position.

Marv didn't pick me first. Obviously, he didn't want to pick his wife first, and I could understand that. But when he didn't pick me the second or third time I began to feel hurt. Here I needed him to be protective and he wasn't making himself available.

He explained later that since I was always complaining about his hogging my ball and telling me what to do, he thought I'd rather be on someone else's team. Normally I'd have liked to be on the team that beat his, but that night my only desire was to survive the evening and go home. Obviously we were not on the same wave length and it hurt.

The next volleyball night things went from bad to worse. Marv spiked a ball across the net with all his might, and it accidentally landed right in my face. For a few moments it really smarted, although I tried not to show it. What really hurt, though, was that Marv never said a word—not "I'm sorry" or "Are you all right?" Nothing. All the way home in the car I was icy cold—not a word did I utter. Finally he asked, "What's the matter?"

"What's the matter?" I retorted. "Oh, nothing. Some tough guy hit me in the face and never bothered to ask how I was. But that's okay. The instructor came over and offered me an ice pack and my teammates seemed concerned."

"Well, I was so embarrassed, I didn't know what to do," Marv explained. "I'm sorry. Are you okay?"

I was in no mood by then for any explanation, reasonable or otherwise. These fun nights of volleyball were getting to be a drag. What happened to the fun of this game, I wondered. Nor could I resist the opportunity to remind Marv of how profusely he had apologized to another player on a different occasion when he had accidentally hit her in the face.

"But that was different," he explained. "You're my wife."

That has always been the worst thing Marv can

possibly say to me. "You're my wife" implies to me that wives don't need to be treated with the same consideration as the rest of the world. I feel that spouses should be treated better than anyone else. This has probably been the area of our biggest dissension, and to this day it is not completely worked out to our satisfaction.

After this course ended, Marv took basketball and I took yoga. I found yoga far more relaxing and enjoyable. Marv liked basketball—until he sprained his ankle.

We know of other couples who also returned to school, some to expand their outlook on the world, some to gain a degree they never quite got around to before. People involved in businesses with quite a limited perspective often find it meaningful to take courses in unrelated subjects. Homemakers sometimes find they get to know their husbands better while sharing a course in ecology or archeology. Going to school together certainly brings new dimensions into a marriage. It is exciting to see your mate become involved in a subject you've never associated him with before. Sometimes you may discover that you or your mate has an intuitive insight into a subject previously unknown.

Another fringe benefit was meeting other students. Over a snack, during break we became acquainted with students of all ages, from all walks of life. Some were the same age as our college freshman daughter, and it was interesting to observe their attitude toward us. We met some people in the same line of work as one of us, and some who lived near us.

Even studying together proved enjoyable. But it always seemed that, when we most needed to stick to our books, that was when we had a million things to discuss with each other.

Incidentally, after a reasonable time had passed, we started playing volleyball together again. And now it's fun again—usually!

CHAPTER FOUR

Are Second Marriages Better?

Is remarriage worth it? A cynic once said that in divorce and remarriage, a person is merely exchanging one set of problems for another.

An extreme statement? Maybe. Yet many couples married for the second time admit there is some truth to that statement. Complicated problems arise in most second marriages. As one man explained:

> When I married the first time, I anticipated a good love relationship (physically and emotionally), planned to establish a secure home for my wife and future children, and looked forward to many years of happiness and fulfillment. Later, when I entered into a second marriage, I still had those same goals, and, in addition, I faced certain complex situations which had to be dealt with. These included maintaining a satisfactory relationship with my children from my first marriage while establishing a meaningful relation-

ship with my new wife's children (now my step-children). It also involved financial involvements with my first wife and my new wife's first husband. I have, I believe, matured in the way I handle such problems, however. I cope rather than run away.

I entered my first marriage with enthusiasm and optimism, blindly expecting love (or the state of being in love) to conquer all. But love did not overcome the problems, and eventually love died.

Therefore, I was determined to analyze every aspect of my relationship with my second husband-to-be before marriage. He was equally cautious. We discussed every topic we could think of and felt very confident of our ability to communicate well. We knew we loved each other, and we felt certain we had covered all potential problem areas. We anticipated a happy and contented future together. Even so, certain problems took us by surprise. They frustrated us, even after all our long talks and very thorough courtship.

However, we were both totally committed to our marriage, and once we got over the initial shock and disappointment, we were willing (usually) to admit our mistakes and keep working at improving our relationship and our famly life.

As we interviewed couples for this book, we were delighted to discover that many couples remarry with the same commitment and optimism we felt. We also discovered that our experiences were very typical of remarried couples.

Unfortunately, statistics regarding remarriage

aren't so encouraging. At the very least, they are contradictory. A surface glance, without considering contributing factors, can be very depressing.

Paul D. Meier, a Christian psychiatrist, claims in an article in *Christian Life* magazine that the divorce rate for second marriages is more than 50% higher than the divorce rate for first marriages. On the other hand, many sociologists, psychologists, and other experts in the family counseling field believe that second marriages have a better chance of succeeding than do first marriages. The determination to "make it work this time" is often quoted as the main explanation.

"Remarriage is the bright side of the divorce picture," states Ann A. Poussaint in her *Ebony* article, "Are Second Marriages Better?" "In it, most people see an opportunity to learn from old mistakes and begin again. People tend to start a second marriage with the determination to 'do it right this time,' as one woman put it."

The available statistics are difficult to check out. They go back to 1969, and there has been an increasing number of divorces and remarriages in the years since then.

Other complicating factors are built into the statistics. First, they cover a wide span of diversified people. There is a correlation between the remarriage failure rate and certain professions. Certain celebrities are known for divorcing and remarrying frequently. Mickey Rooney and Elizabeth Taylor, each married seven times, are only two examples.

Other professions are also prone to marriage failure. The temptations and opportunities in certain jobs are greater than in others. Truckers, gone from home for days at a time, become lonely and are tempted to take their marriage vows more lightly. Spouses of sailors and fishermen who are away at sea for long periods of time may seek out other companionship during long absences. Naturally, this isn't true of everyone in any profession, but sometimes work factors do play havoc with the marital relationship. A person whose first marriage ended in divorce because he was "married to his job," for example, may run into similar trouble in a subsequent marriage unless the problem is resolved.

Another explanation for the high divorce rate among the remarried comes from Dr. Norman J. Levy, a psychiatrist and professor at the Postgraduate Center for Mental Health in New York. When interviewed by Carmel Berman Reingold, he stated, "There are people who are narcissistic . . . wanting to be told that they are charming, witty, clever, and wanting to have everything they want all the time." Such people quit easily when things don't go just the way they want. They are the exception rather than the norm, but they, too, are included in the statistics.

We know too about financial extremes—people who marry and divorce to obtain financial benefits, or who live such deprived lives that getting married becomes simply something to do until something or someone more interesting comes along.

Here again, research is incomplete and often contradictory. Mary Jo Bane, author of *Here to Stay,* gives an example of how one study contradicts a second. She describes available reports on the effects of women's economic situations on their decision to remarry.

> One study found that better-off women were more likely to remarry, suggesting that their incomes made them more attractive marriage partners. Another study found they were less likely to remarry, suggesting that women may weigh the decision to remarry more carefully when they are supporting themselves adequately or that men feel threatened by financially independent women.

She suggests that the source of women's income may be an important factor. Women receiving large welfare checks or taking advantage of improved employment opportunities may account for some leveling off of remarriage rates.

A woman who gains a bankbook, house, and car from her divorce may become particularly vulnerable. Feeling inadequate as a result of her divorce—because each partner, no matter who initiates the divorce, tends to suffer some feelings of inadequacy—she may fail to realize that a newly divorced man, having lost those same material things to his ex-wife, may believe the easiest way to get on his feet financially is to marry someone else's ex-wife who "got everything" as a result of divorce.

Certain personality types have a high failure rate because of specific problems, such as excessive gambling, alcoholism, drug addiction, or serious emotional disturbances.

A particularly sad statistic points out the trend for

people to divorce one spouse because of a particular problem and then turn around and remarry someone else with the same problem. Widowed people, too, may fall into this habit. I know of one woman who for years endured marriage to a chronic hypochondriac. When he was killed in an automobile accident, some of her friends breathed a sigh of relief on her behalf, until she turned around and married another man with the identical behavior pattern. Psychologists believe this indicates a need in her—perhaps to mother a spouse or to be a martyr.

During the years I was divorced, I often read statistics about remarriage patterns among divorced persons. Most indicated that four out of five divorced men remarry and three out of four divorced women remarry. Within five years, 75% of all divorced people remarry. Men usually remarry within two years after their divorce, women usually not until four or five years after their divorce.

When I first got divorced, I was certain I would not be part of the 75% of divorced people who remarried within five years. I didn't intend ever to remarry. As it turned out, however, both my husband and I remarried within the average period of time; my husband within two years and I within five years.

My first reaction after reading these statistics, that they would never apply to me, was typical. Most people, immediately after getting divorced or being widowed, aren't open to the idea of remarriage. It isn't until they pass through a series of cycles (similar to grief cycles) that they begin to think positively about remarriage. There are always exceptions, of course, including those who end one marriage in order to marry someone else.

There is much disagreement on the importance of the ages of the couple. Because most first marriages take place early in life, more first marriages pair a man and woman of similar ages. With second marriages, there are numerous examples of younger women marrying older men, and recently an increasing number of successful marriages between younger men and older women.

Dame Agatha Christie described her marriage to a younger man in *Time* magazine. Her first marriage ended when, as she stoically put it, "My husband found a young woman." On a trip to the Middle East in 1930, Dame Agatha found Max Mallowan, 14 years her junior, who was excavating on the site of ancient Ur. "An archaeologist is the best husband any woman can have," she noted before their 25th anniversary. "The older she gets, the more interested he is in her." The Mallowans were married 45 years when she died.

There are many other successful second marriages to look to for encouragement: Gerald and Betty Ford, Catherine Marshall and Leonard LeSourd, Dale Evans Rogers and Roy Rogers, to name just a few. Like almost everything else in life, second marriages bring no guarantees. There's a risk, but also a great deal of hope and optimism.

According to these somewhat unreliable statistics, couples in their second marriage are less likely to outgrow each other, a real threat to young couples entering their first marriage. Statistics indicate that marriages in which the husband is under 22 years of age and the wife under 20 have twice the possibility of ending in divorce as marriages between older couples. Often, as young couples mature, they develop into two very different people. (Here again I find myself running with the statistics; both my first husband and I were younger than the quoted ages.)

Among those couples I interviewed, the idea of their outgrowing each other did not arise. Nobody mentioned it, and I didn't catch the mildest hint that it might be an area of dissension. By the time of second marriage, most persons have had the opportunity to mature and develop in their areas of interest.

The couples often commented that they believed they had gained helpful insights from their previous mistakes and were thus better equipped for marriage. They intended to use their past to advantage in their effort to build a better marital relationship this time around. One woman commented:

> My first marriage more or less provided a training period for the second. I know that for one thing, I appreciate this husband so much more— I am very grateful that I have a kind, loving husband. Also, I believe I have learned to give-and-take more; that is, I am more willing to give of myself this time around.

These and similar comments clearly indicate that the important difference between first marriages and later marriages was certainly not that there are fewer problems. Instead, it is the spirit of determination, maturity, and commitment with which marriage is entered into and with which problems are handled.

Second-timers rarely enter marriage expecting to change their partner to fit their own preferred mold. They have usually learned via their first marriage that this seldom works. Second-timers I interviewed were obviously willing to try to improve their own behavior and personality traits.

Most persons discover after their first marriage ends that it is essential to tear up and throw out their old "loser" script for living and rewrite a new "winner" script. Some find healing and help through their faith in Christ, supported by their pastor and congregation. (Sadly, some had not felt welcome or wanted in their church.) Others find help in sharing groups, either through their church or organizations such as Parents Without Partners or Faith at Work.

Jack Cushman said, "I don't believe any couple can ever really *solve* all their problems. Instead, I feel they can and must learn to *cope* with some things and make the best of them."

Jack had been somewhat depressed after his first marriage ended in divorce, mainly because he missed his kids. For a while, he buried himself in books on positive thinking. He wanted to improve those qualities that worked against him in his first marriage. Now, in his second marriage, he tries to use a positive approach whenever possible and put to use the lessons learned from his past mistakes.

Jack met his second wife, Marilyn, at a Parents Without Partners meeting. She had started attending about a year after her first husband died. Both were enthusiastic about the fellowship and support they received from this group. In fact, she mentioned that they still keep in touch with the group and some of the couples who were married after meeting there.

One of the most remarkable things I discovered in interviewing people who are remarried was that, no matter how unique their particular situation (and each one was very different), certain similarities, mostly in their attitude, stood out. I found most couples to be absolutely honest and open—completely lacking in phoniness. Apparently they learned in their first marriages that openness and honesty work far better in the long run.

I was especially able to identify with some honest comments made by Loni Whitcraft. When I asked her what she found to be the biggest area of stress in her second marriage, she replied, "My strong-willed, stubborn, opinionated, and somewhat selfish personality!" (I could have made that identical statement myself, had I Loni's honesty.) She continued:

> However, I was not aware that this was the root cause. All that I saw was a jealous, possessive husband who wanted to keep me in a cage all to himself and stifle my creative urges. I was also unaware of my sophisticated methods of subtle nagging and belittling my husband. My attitude of martyrdom and subtle nagging turned my gentle, loving husband off, and away from me. I was puzzled! I believed I was *doing* everything a good wife should, and this was the way he repaid me.
>
> Unfortunately these are the same attitudes I brought out of my first marriage. Then I learned some very important lessons. The Lord led me to several extremely good books: *Do I Have to Be Me?* by Lloyd Ahlem, *Hide or Seek* by James

Dobson, *Knowing God* by J. I. Packer, and *Fruit of the Spirit* by John Sanderson. He used these books to reveal myself to myself. Eventually I was able to put into proper perspective the person I was and the person I wanted to be. As I became secure in his agape love, I became liberated from myself to be the kind of wife and woman Jesus intended me to be.

Loni learned the danger of entering a second marriage without dealing with the problems that brought about the breakup of the first marriage.

According to Dr. Walter Johnson, head of Family Studies Center at Sangamon State University, an extremely important factor which can tremendously affect remarriage is the amount of time between marriages. It takes time to adjust to what Dr. Johnson refers to as the "excruciating decision of divorce." Himself divorced and remarried, Dr. Johnson says:

It is especially tough on individuals who are the first in their family to go through a divorce. Divorce, for whatever reasons, is still looked upon as a failure. This stigma of a loser makes it very difficult to adjust, and particularly difficult to look at oneself objectively. We often rationalize the need for divorce by pointing out the other person's deficiencies. It wasn't *our* fault; it was the other person's fault. We did everything we could to save the marriage, but the other person did not help. Therefore, we feel we have the right to blame them. This is often followed by a vindictiveness toward our former spouse we did not know we were even capable of. If we have not worked our way out of that stage, obviously this attitude can be projected into our new marriage.

As divorced persons, according to Dr. Johnson, our ego has been damaged, our pride has been hurt, and sometimes we begin to feel ugly—not necessarily in a physical sense, but simply ugly about ourselves. Therefore, we are particularly vulnerable. One of the easiest ways to restore feelings of self-esteem is to reassure ourselves that we are attractive to the opposite sex. A common, accessible means of doing this is going to singles bars—which Dr. Johnson claims are better named divorcee bars. People whose marriages end often turn first to bars for companionship, gratification, and sex without commitment.

This is dangerous, according to Johnson, because "often you run into someone who is kind to you or who understands you, and before you know it you are involved. In this stage where you need reassuring and confidence, you may be so encouraged by these factors that you tend to overlook many other elements that you might have seen if you had more time between marriages to work out these insecurities." This rushing into a second marriage may partially account for the high rate of divorce in remarriage.

People who have lost a spouse through death are not immune to some of these problems. A spouse satisfies many needs, and loss of a mate's support is difficult to adjust to. Jane Gunther, in an article titled "How to Survive Widowhood" *(Reader's Digest,* June 1975), says: "For me, the hardest of the benefits my husband had provided for me to do without was psychological support. I am a shy person. My husband gave me a confidence that made me feel comfortable in any social situation, and his approval sustained me in private as well."

Persons who suddenly lose this approval and support through death of a spouse are in a situation similar to those who feel rejected through divorce. They can easily close their eyes to the faults and differences in a new person they meet, if that new person is able to provide for some basic needs of the hurting person. Once they establish a relationship with a new person of the opposite sex, they're likely to stick with it, even if there are serious problems, rather than face losing another supportive person.

Newly single persons go through grief cycles very similar to those experienced by persons who lose a spouse in death. If, with the help of friends, clergy, and counselors, they can work through these first grief cycles, they will enter into new relationships with the opposite sex in a much more mature, stable, secure manner. Time is essential.

Once newly single persons are able to look at their present circumstances as a second chance, an opportunity for self-discovery, a chance to start living all over again, they are ready to make friendships with the opposite sex based on healthy give-and-take.

Most second-timers realize it takes much more than romantic love to create a satisfying marriage. It takes hard work and a sincere desire to make it a success. Persons entering a second marriage are more realistic, usually, than idealistic, younger first-timers, who often believe love can overcome all manner of problems.

This doesn't have to mean, however, that remarried people are or should be less romantic. The couples we interviewed offered a wide variety of opinions on this subject. Doug and Hellen Dawson have experienced more romance and fun in this marriage than in their previous ones. They delight in the romantic element of their relationship.

On Saturdays, Doug gets up early and spends the morning at his office. He encourages Hellen to "sleep in." Before leaving home, he makes a pot of coffee, sets out her cup and saucer, and writes a little note which he tucks into her cup. She enjoys this so much that one morning, when she really had reasons to get up early with him, she decided to stay in bed until he left, because she didn't want to miss out on the love note. The minute he was out of the door, she scrambled into the kitchen to fetch her note.

Doug had also "romanced" Hellen by keeping her supplied with fresh flowers and interesting charms for the charm bracelet he purchased for her on their first Christmas.

Romance is obviously effective in their relationship, as one can tell by their comfortable enjoyment of each other. Many marriages have broken up because romance has died—and evidently neither mate cared enough to bring it back into the relationship. In *What Wives Wish Their Husbands Knew about Women*, Dr. James Dobson says:

> If I had the power to communicate only one message to every family in America, I would specify the importance of romantic love to every aspect of feminine existence. It provides the foundation for a woman's self-esteem, her joy in

living, and her sexual responsiveness. Therefore, the vast number of men who are involved in bored, tired marriages — and find themselves locked out of the bedroom—should know where the trouble possibly lies. Real love can melt an iceberg.

The subject of communication came up frequently in my interviews. Most couples had learned, usually from disappointing first marriages, that there is no substitute for open communication. (This is not to be confused with open marriage—which was not recommended by anyone I interviewed.) While they might have "beat around the bush" and left some things unsaid in their first marriages, they had decided together to avoid playing guessing games in their new marriage and to spell things out, even when this involves more effort and confrontations that might be disagreeable.

Like Marv and me, other couples had also decided before getting remarrried to talk together about what each wanted out of the new marriage—without compromising themselves and playing a role just to please (or hold on to) the other.

Dr. Aaron Rutledge, in his column in the Chicago *Sun Times,* says that sometimes one person unconsciously decides to first find out what the other person wants in a marriage partner and then tries to *be* that. But, he points out, these roles may not be true to the basic self. In other words, it becomes role playing. How long can you play the game before you sacrifice your own person?

Couples entering second marriages usually have

learned from experiences in their first marriages that pretending doesn't work. They have learned that trying too hard to be all a spouse desires can result in growing anger because their own needs are not being met. Many people fear that if they let their spouse know their real self, the spouse will be displeased and might even reject them. In *Why Am I Afraid to Tell You Who I Am?* John Powell says:

> If friendship and human love are to mature between any two persons, there must be absolute and honest mutual revelation; this kind of self-revelation can be achieved only through what we have called "gut-level" communication. There is no other way, and all the reasons which we adduce to rationalize our cover-ups and dishonesty must be seen as delusions. It would be much better for me to tell you how I really feel about you than to enter into the stickiness and discomfort of a phoney relationship. Dishonesty always has a way of coming back to haunt and trouble us. Even if I should have to tell you that I do not admire or love you emotionally, it would be much better than trying to deceive you and having to pay the ultimate price of all such deception, your greater hurt and mine.

Perhaps it was this kind of honest communication that Hellen Dawson was referring to when I asked her what she most enjoys doing with Doug.

"Talking!" she said. "Usually we get into conversations at the dinner table. We may sit down for a 15-minute meal and end up talking two hours."

"The best part of it is that neither one of us tries to con the other," injected Doug. "I am really not interested in trying to sell Hellen anything."

"We have a lot of fun in our marriage," Hellen continued, "and talking is part of it." With a twinkle in her eye, she added, "Of course, we find that sex is a lot of fun, too. I remember reading a statement about sex that you might want to include in your book: 'If sex is right, it is 10% of your marriage. If it is unsatisfactory, it is 90% of your marriage.'"

"That's right," Doug emphasized. "I've thought about that for a long time. And we've passed it on to people who react by saying, 'Wow, is that ever true.'"

Dr. Walter Johnson of Sangamon State University believes second-timers don't always learn as much as they could from their first mistakes. He even recommends that a couple contemplating a second marriage seriously consider drawing up a marital contract. He does not mean they should consider what would happen if they divorce. Rather, he recommends a contract as a means of opening up to the other person before the marriage. He believes that, during the courting process, some people are even more likely than with their first marriage to put their best foot forward. Someone whose first marriage didn't work may be particularly cautious not to alarm the other individual. They do so at a cost—they do not let the other individual see them as they really are. As a consequence, the other person does not have a true picture of how the future mate will react in particular situations. Dr. Johnson believes that if you cannot talk out these situations before the marriage and work through some method which is mutually satisfactory for arbitrating disputes that arise, then it is not time to get married and it may even be that this is not the person to marry.

Johnson says that if you are uneasy about reactions of the prospective spouse or if you have doubts about marriage, "then you'd better not do it." He thinks one of the best ways to check whether you're ready for marriage is to write up a marital contract which both of you can sign. "If you are not comfortable with it and you don't tell that to the other person, you're asking for trouble," he warns.

"I am a believer in awareness groups," Johnson says. "I feel that a person contemplating a second marriage could benefit so much from becoming involved in such a group—possibly at first alone and later with the potential spouse."

Hellen and Doug Dawson met each other in an awareness group. Although romance is important to their relationship, their realistic approach to marriage is also important. They believe in open and honest communication and they refuse to play roles just to please each other or society.

When asked what their major adjustment problem was, and whether this type of open communication helped, they agreed it had not only helped but eventually was the method by which the problem was resolved.

Doug and Hellen both "wore the pants" in their first marriages. The two dominating personalities sometimes come together in a head-on collision.

Hellen explains that Doug assumed they would do things his way. "I rebelled," she said. "I found myself literally screaming at Doug, telling him that I must have my own identity."

Hellen believes she needs to work at being less dominating. She is willing to become more aware of her assertiveness and to try to change her behavior to some degree. Doug realizes he needs to share decision-making with Hellen. But working together has taken deliberate effort and a willingness to bend.

A divorced mother of two describes a similar situation. She is engaged to a divorced man who has custody of his three children. Both of them had been operating for some time as head of a household, managing their own lives and those of their children quite efficiently. Occasionally their independent natures collided.

Since I had been divorced five years before remarrying, I, too, had become quite independent and self-sufficient. It wasn't long before Marv and I ran into disagreements about routine household chores, such as auditing our bank statements. I had "always" done it one way, Marv had "always" done it another way. I honestly still believe my method is more accurate, and Marv still honestly believes his way is. He usually balances the checkbook, however, since he is better with figures.

How do minor disagreements in second marriages differ from those in first marriages? When a first-time couple marries, they establish habits together. They may shop around before they decide where they prefer to buy their gas or groceries. They may try a number of different ways to budget and save money

71

before agreeing on a particular financial program that works best for them.

But when blending two persons who, in different teams, have each previously worked through these processes and who have each experienced some degree of success in managing a household, then compromising and bending are required. Little things can seem very big if you feel your way has been "put down." This situation often breeds the feeling: "She doesn't think my way of doing things has any merit. She's so sure her way is best that, in her opinion, my way seems inferior." Idealistically, second-timers could come up with a new way of budgeting and an entirely different set of stores to shop at. But such alternatives are often inferior or just plain unworkable.

Financial obligations cause considerable problems in second marriages. Couples with no children from previous marriages seem to have the least financial troubles. Problems often arise from a spouse paying child support for children from a previous marriage. As Dr. Wes Brun put it, "My wife and I could live considerably better if I didn't have to pay child support. Of course, I wouldn't have it any other way. But it is in this area that my first marriage most acutely invades my second marriage." (Dr. Brun is coordinator of parish services at the Community Pastoral Counseling Center at Lutheran General Hospital in Park Ridge.)

One woman, who had not been previously married, says she struggles constantly not to resent the child-support payments that are sent to her husband's child by his first marriage. While she had known about this before their marriage and certainly realized it was a necessity, she often finds herself thinking of all the things that money could buy for their two children from this marriage.

Frequent problems also arise when a natural parent caring for the children is not receiving any or adequate child-support payments from the former spouse. It is very disillusioning that stepfathers are usually assumed to be responsible for stepchildren with whom they live, on application forms for college scholarships, for instance. Yet, if their spouse (the children's natural parent) dies, they will almost certainly *not* be awarded custody of the children. Unless there has been a legal adoption, which is rare when the natural parent is alive and well, the court usually returns the children to the other natural parent, even if this parent has abused or neglected the children.

Often stepparents would be delighted to adopt the children, especially if the natural parent has abandoned them financially and emotionally. Yet frequently natural parents refuse to sign adoption papers, not because they care about the children, but because of emotional unstability or for selfish reasons, possibly to get revenge on the former spouse. The courts are extremely hesitant to rule in behalf of stepparents in such situations. This can be very disappointing to stepparents who have loved and cared for their stepchildren as their own.

I remember reading of two young men who went together to a lawyer's office to arrange for one man to adopt the other man's little girl. The natural father said that, much as he loved the youngster, he knew she would have a more secure life if he would allow the stepfather to adopt her and give her the same name as her mother. But such self-sacrifice is rare. Much more common are natural parents with the get-even, selfish attitude who keep the children legally bound even though they have little interest in the children's welfare.

Occasionally a stepfather is faithfully sending child-support payments to children from his first marriage and at the same time providing a comfortable home for his stepchildren and children from his new marriage, while the father of his stepchildren neglects making support payments. It is difficult for him not to project his frustration about this unfair situation onto his new wife and his stepchildren. He may tend to "put down" the natural parent. According to Pastor Ken Stangeland, this only succeeds in "making a martyr of the natural parent" by putting the child in the position of defending the natural parent's irresponsibility. Stangeland explains:

> The way the stepparent handles such situations, whether he becomes an actor or reactor, will have a great deal of influence on his relationship with his stepchildren. If a mature stepparent can look ahead to the long-range goals of the household, even though some situations *are* undoubtedly unfair, the child will probably react to this sign of stability and eventually respond and respect it.

Marriages entered into primarily for economic

comfort do not appear to have a high degree of success. This is true among older couples as well as younger. Janet Sherbin, in "Why Older Marriages Work" (*Modern Maturity,* Feb./March 1977), tells of two older women who had watched their resources drain and married wealthy men out of desperation. "They rejoice in their financial comfort," Sherbin reported, "but lament their emotional disappointment."

Sherbin interviewed 24 couples, all of whom had been previously married. Nearly all the couples had some income besides Social Security—pensions or savings or part-time jobs. She also discovered that many of the couples agreed before marriage to keep any money they brought into the marriage in their own names and to pool subsequent income. "This arrangement works well!" she comments.

Some of the couples we interviewed had made similar agreements before remarriage. For example, if a spouse had died, it was agreed that the inheritance would be earmarked for the children's college expenses.

Often couples neglect giving adequate thought to financial matters, in case either dies prematurely. Then a first mate's unexpected death catches survivors unprepared. A woman may be totally uninformed regarding financial matters of the household. She then has not only her grief to cope with; she also has to quickly assume the financial responsibilities.

Many courses are available to women who want to learn how to handle family finances. Local YWCAs

75

often conduct helpful seminars geared to help women prepare for such crises in their lives. Unfortunately, those who believe something like that could never happen to them pass up opportunities to prepare themselves.

I also believe in the importance of women (whether employed outside the home or not) being adequately insured in case of their unexpected and early death. I am disappointed when insurance salespersons stress the necessity of insuring the man and forget the financial loss that would be felt should the woman die, especially if there are youngsters in the home.

Financial situations of remarried couples vary widely. In some cases, finances soon become a major area of stress, while in other marriages finances are arranged smoothly. Some couples are financially secure. Others have suffered heavy financial losses as a result of divorce.

While Marv and I both have sound jobs and are making comfortable salaries, both of us lost through divorce our first homes and accumulated savings. At the age of 36 we found ourselves starting all over again with house payments. This time we paid a much higher price than for our first homes because of skyrocketing prices and higher rates of interest. It was hard not to think about the houses we had owned earlier, each of which had mortgage payments which were about a third of what now confronts us monthly. However, there is a positive side.

Two months before I met Marv, I had an opportunity to rent a house with an option to buy. This locked up the purchase price for two years. A small portion of my monthly rental payments was allocated towards the purchase price, should I exercise my option.

I felt certain at the time that the Lord had guided me to this home. As a divorced woman with three children, with no money for a down payment, I had few opportunities to get out of the renting bind. Renting was a financial dead end, and it had been very discouraging. We had been living in the house we were renting only six months when the owners were transferred by his company back to the area. Naturally, they were anxious to get back into their own home, which we also liked very much. We enjoyed the neighborhood, the nearby school was excellent, and our babysitter was two doors down, so we were especially disappointed.

Just a few days before we had to move, an opportunity came to rent with option our present home. It was only two blocks from the home we needed to leave and, considering the available homes I had looked at, weekends and evenings, for months, I felt it was a very good deal.

Since getting married, Marv and I have bought the home. While it still needs a lot of work, it has already increased in market value, which convinces me that God did have a hand in directing me to this house. I was also glad that I had not lived in it with my previous husband, which would have complicated the situation, both financially and emotionally, when Marv and I decided to marry. Our two salaries combined barely enable us to meet the needs of our three children (one with three more years of college and two more years of orthodontic work to go). It will be a number of years before we start building a nest egg. However, both of us knew when we made our individual decisions to divorce that we would experience a considerable financial loss, and we were prepared for that unpleasant aspect of divorce.

In her book *Remarriage,* Carmel Berman Reingold asks whether money problems can cause a second marriage to end. She answers herself with a vehement "Yes, if the marriage's foundation was basically financial." But she adds, "When people have remarried, not because of external or superficial things, but because of a sense of love and relatedness, money —or problems stemming from a lack of it—will not destroy a marriage."

Reingold relates an incident which touches on both finances and the courts' unfair treatment of persons involved in second marriages. Maggie had been widowed without children for 10 years before marrying a divorced man with two children. She worked and contributed her fair share to the household expenses. She and Frank had been married five years when his business took a downhill turn and he found he'd have to borrow money to keep up alimony and child-support payments. He applied to the court to lower alimony payments. During the first hearing in family court, the lawyer representing his first wife asked, "How can this man ask to have alimony payments lowered, when he owns a mansion in East Hampton?"

The truth of the matter was that Maggie had purchased a tiny vacation cottage before marrying Frank. She made all the payments on it. She said, "Look, Frank, what is Mona's (his first wife) is Mona's and what is yours is Mona's but what is mine is mine."

Maggie brought all the necessary papers to court to prove her ownership of the home. She was stunned when told that she wouldn't be allowed in the hearing room: "This doesn't concern you."

Even though she never got her fair day in court, the judge did lower alimony payments when her husband brought in his IRS records to prove that his business was losing money.

Tragically, this situation is not unusual. In addition to the courts, other federal and state agencies reflect paradoxical attitudes toward remarried couples.

Learning to account to another person again about one's spending can be a difficult adjustment, especially after each individual has experienced some years of "free spending." Hellen Dawson recalls the time when she went out on her lunch hour and purchased three outfits. When she and Doug were returning home from work together, she told him, "I bought three outfits today."

"How much did they cost?" Doug asked.

Hellen found herself giving a lower price than she had paid. Immediately she caught herself. She said, "I just lied to you," and she told Doug the correct amount. "If I hadn't leveled with him then, that could have been the beginning of a lying relationship."

Finances can do a lot to make or break the marriage. How much money a couple has is less important than how they handle it and whether they agree on the method of handling it.

Another difficult adjustment to make in second marriages is handling memories of a deceased spouse or of a marriage ended by divorce.

"I get sick and tired of hearing about my wife's saintly first husband," one man confided. "No one could have been as good as she remembers him to be. As a matter of fact, I have been told by others who knew him that he wasn't all that fantastic as she remembers." His wife's sentimental and distorted memories are devastating to this man, who is trying to be himself and not a carbon copy of his wife's first husband.

Doug Dawson says, "I don't remember today how my foot hurt two years ago. I know it hurt, but I don't remember or feel just how painful it was at the time. This is the same way with my first marriage. I remember there were problems, but I don't always remember just how painful they were."

"I want to remember only the good things about my first wife and forget the bad times," another man said. This was devastating to his new wife, who felt haunted by an image of perfection and often wondered why her husband ever divorced his first wife.

Yes, memories can affect a new marriage—numerous experiences related by marriage couples clearly point this out.

One woman tells of feeling hesitant to express her views on a certain subject because her husband, during their courtship, had often emphasized how it had irritated him when his wife got on that same subject. On the other hand, she felt she was compromising herself and her values by keeping quiet.

A man who is "all thumbs" with handyman chores around the house feels inadequate when his wife reminds him of all the things her talented first husband made and repaired around the house in which they now live.

I felt frustrated one day by a comment Marv made when a neighbor was out busily weeding her beautiful flower garden. He said, supposedly in jest, "Now, *that* is what a good wife should do!" He knew that, though I would find leisurely work in our yard relaxing, my full-time job, three children, and freelance writing left no time for gardening. I was acutely aware that, in addition to keeping her house immaculate and baking well, Marv's first wife had been very handy at gardening.

I believe now that I perceived this situation somewhat out of context and felt overly threatened by it. But such a reaction is typical for second-timers who are trying to please a new spouse but live with that skeleton in the closet. When I describe this experience to people who are single or in their first marriage, they say, "You were being ridiculous, weren't you?" But when I describe it to second-timers, most often they respond, "I know what you mean."

Naturally, a pleasant memory of the first marriage occasionally flits across one's mind, even if the marriage ended on a sour note. After all, at one time the couple enjoyed each other or they never would have married. A certain vacation spot brings back memories of the first honeymoon, or a house looks like the home of former in-laws. Such memories are normal. It is the extremes that jeopardize a new relationship.

Some second-timers tell me they make deliberate efforts to brush away memories of their first marriage. They emphasize this is better than allowing the mind to reminisce excessively, which they believe to be destructive to both themselves and their new spouse.

A woman who had been widowed and has remarried a widower says she doesn't believe she could have married a divorced man. If her husband's ex-wife were still living, she would seem more "real." She can live with memories of a dead person, but she isn't sure how she would deal with memories of a woman only a phone call away.

Others who have trouble with memories say it is just as possible to be jealous of a dead person. They may not have expected these feelings when they first remarried, but they soon learned that death raises many ex-spouses to "instant sainthood" in the eyes of many survivors.

Marilyn Cushman has realistically explained to her children that just because her first husband (the children's natural father) died, they shouldn't think the marriage had been perfect. They had their ups and downs, just as she and her second husband occasionally have.

A steady diet of feeling sorry for an ex-spouse is another detriment to a healthy new relationship. A new spouse can become sick and tired of their wife or husband feeling sorry for their first mate, showing that their emotional involvement with that person evidently had not been adequately severed. Some such feelings are probably to be expected in the early stages after divorce, especially by the person initiating the divorce, but sometimes they indicate that guilt feelings have not been dealt with adequately. No one benefits from being felt sorry for, especially not the first spouse. A person rarely learns to become self-sufficient while leaning on a crutch, and an overly sympathetic ex-spouse can easily become that crutch.

Sometimes a person entering a new marriage is troubled by unhappy, even tragic memories. Florence Pauls discovered that her resentment and bitterness eased when she decided to pray for her first husband and his parents. She has found that one of the most meaningful things to her and her new husband Ferdi is praying together. She explained how each morning, while Ferdi has his breakfast, she reads a short devotional thought for the day. Then they pray together—about their own needs, but especially about other people who they know have special needs. The impact this has on their marriage, according to Florence, is beautiful.

In "Why Me, God?" *(Reader's Digest,* September 1976), Leola Mae Harmon tells a most poignant story about how second marriage can erase the hurts of the first marriage.

At the age of 23, this pretty, fun-loving gal was on her way to duties as an Air Force nurse. She was five months pregnant and feeling on top of the world.

Tragedy struck when a giant trailer truck swung into her lane from behind an oncoming school bus. The impact threw her against the windshield, then jerked her back and slammed her face against the steering column, finally hurtling her through the glass. The effect on her face was devastating. Her child was stillborn three days later.

The first time she looked in a mirror she was repulsed by the swollen, discolored, toothless mass of tissue that was obviously only about one-third of her face. She reports, "The revulsion I felt then had already been experienced by my husband, an ex-Air Force corpsman." As he stood by her bed, she could see in his eyes that, though she still lived, *his* wife had died. There was grief on his face, but it was for the pretty, fun-loving girl he'd lost on that highway. What he saw was a stomach-wrenching stranger. Without a sound or touch, he left the room. The moment of unspoken goodbye was later confirmed by divorce.

During those first days and months and years after her accident, Leola received devoted care from a plastic surgeon, Dr. James O. Stallings. While she was still in the emergency room, he had put a firm hand on her shoulder and in a low, gentle voice had said, "Hang on. You're going to make it." Leola says, "And I believed him."

This same voice was commanding and firm as Dr. Stallings ordered the emergency room staff into activity. It continued to be gentle but firm throughout Leola's many operations, face reconstruction, dental surgery, and years of touch-up work. As she battled against hopelessness and depression, Leola found strength in Dr. Stallings' way of saying, without words, "You're special, and don't you forget it."

After a while, Leola had come to anticipate Jim Stallings' surgical miracles, but then came one miracle she had never expected. One day Dr. Stallings told her, "Leo, I think we should get married." She was stunned. "Doctor . . . ." Then she laughed. When he asked why, she replied, "You've just proposed to me—and I can't bring myself to use your first name!" Then she happily accepted his proposal.

Their story provides a poignant example of how rich and meaningful a second marriage can be when based not on financial security or looks or material consideration, but on a deep, inward relationship.

CHAPTER FIVE

Considering Counseling

Many couples decide (some even before remarrying) to seek professional guidance. This can be especially valuable when children are involved and the marriage brings about a blending of families.

One man says emphatically that the most powerful piece of advice he can offer to a couple entering a second marriage is to secure professional help. He was speaking out of his own experience. He realizes many years later that he often made poor decisions when his children had a conflict with his second wife. Too often he took the side of his children, partly because he felt protective toward them since the death of their natural mother. He seldom maintained a united front with his new wife. He sees now that he not only caused his wife unnecessary pain; he also alienated his children from their stepmother. As the years passed, things smoothed over somewhat, but he is now convinced that many of the early problems could have been avoided, had they sought professional guidance.

Lillian Messinger found among the 70 remarried couples she interviewed problems aplenty — often new ones that the couples were unprepared to handle. She concludes that the new partners desperately need education. Unfortunately, she reports, our culture has not yet evolved traditions providing remarried parents with a model of appropriate behavior.

What is the right kind of help? Those seeking professional counsel have numerous options. Some are excellent, some mediocre, and some may do more harm than good. It is of utmost importance to be extremely selective. Never take the first counselor who comes to mind. Check around. Personal references are helpful, but each couple must remember that their needs are unique. What may have been effective for one couple may not be helpful to another.

Marv and I were discouraged to discover that quite a few of the couples we interviewed had found out the hard way that many professional counselors have only a vague concept of the problems inherent in second marriages. Many counselors underestimate the complexity of the situation. Some treat a second marriage exactly the same as a first marriage. Others openly admit they feel ill-equipped, because of lack of information, to counsel partners in remarriage.

Dr. Walter Johnson shares his own experiences in remarriage:

Nothing in my background of experiences or education totally prepared me for the emotional upheaval brought about by divorce and subsequent remarriage ... and I find this true of most of the couples I counsel.

Unless the person has gone through divorce and remarriage, I don't think they can completely understand the emotionality of the situation. You sometimes hear the old argument that if a person wants to be a doctor and learns how to fix fractured limbs, he doesn't have to go out and break his own to do so. But I think there is a lot to say on the emotional side for having experienced some of that. You can relate to what others have written, but unless you feel it yourself, it becomes extremely difficult to empathize and to put yourself in that position.

Professionals in marriage and divorce counseling tend to counsel passively rather than actively. A person having difficulties in a marital situation goes to a professional because they would like assistance; they need help and are seeking answers. They don't always get that. What they sometimes get is a person who sits there and listens to them.

This allows them to vent some of their frustrations—but they also need reinforcement. They need direction. They need to know whether these emotions happen only to them or if they are common. I believe we need to take a new position and have more active counseling, both in reassurance and in telling people when what they are saying may be harmful to their relationship.

Counseling cannot be totally positive when a person comes in, sits down, relates episodes or feelings for 40 minutes and leaves thinking their reasoning is correct. I believe it is wrong to allow a patient to come in and simply constantly reassure him, saying "That's right" or "I hear what you are saying." It may be that the other person isn't right. You may have to force that person to question their motives, to question their emotions. And if you don't do that, it seems to me the counselor is not really counseling.

I asked Dr. Wes Brun, "How can a person know whether the counseling they are receiving is good or not so good?" He responded:

You are asking a very profound question. This is certainly an issue that still needs study. In fact, it is a subject on which psychotherapists themselves disagree.

Counseling cannot be all things to all people. However, I believe the patient should remember that he is the consumer and he is buying a service. If the experience of counseling results in his feeling tremendous dissatisfaction or if the sessions have a consistently negative effect, I believe this should be looked at seriously.

I would suggest the individual or family receiving counseling talk these feelings over with someone they trust, such as their pastor. It may well be that the type of counseling they are receiving is not meeting their needs.

Of course, the key to successful counseling lies in the skill of the therapist. Just as in every other profession, there are highly skilled persons and less effective persons. On the other hand, if one has gone through a succession of counselors and still is discontented, I would then be inclined to believe the problem lies in the patient rather than the therapist.

A couple seeking professional guidance must decide whether to get help within the Christian counseling field or from secular resources. Years ago, it was commonly believed that the few Christian counselors available were unprofessional and inexperienced. Today, great strides have been made by Christians in the field of counseling. Churches have recognized their members' needs for professional help. And more and more Christians are becoming convinced that the church should take the initiative in counseling its own members as well as those outside the church who come for help.

Jay Adams, professor of practical theology at Westminster Theological Seminary, thinks that psychotherapy is the biggest deception since Jacob tricked Esau. He asserts that emotional difficulties are caused by sinful behavior and attitudes and that the correct prescription for handling all such problems is to be found in the Bible. According to him (and others in his school of thinking), every problem can be solved by searching Scriptures.

I have no interest in debating that issue. I only know that, when confronted with certain problems and issues, I need all the help I can get, and I do not usually have adequate knowledge to interpret Scriptures to fit my situation. I need the expertise of those better equipped to objectively identify my problems and mistakes and direct me toward finding the best answer for me and my family.

When I have spiritual questions or problems, I immediately seek help from my pastor. I am fortunate because my pastor is a trained professional. Many pastors today are trained in pastoral counseling.

Gary Collins, professor of pastoral psychology and counseling at Trinity Divinity School in Deerfield, Illinois, points out that there are, in the minds of many, two kinds of sins: acceptable and unacceptable. To many pastors, even today, the "sin of divorce" is unacceptable and carries a stigma which is not projected onto other reformed "sinners." When seeking help, be alert to those who try to make you feel excessively guilty.

In "Divorce and Remarriage: Is It God's Permissive Will?" *(Evangelical Visitor)*, author Dwight Replogle recommends the separation of remarried persons: "Isn't it just plain common sense that since remarriage is adultery and adultery is sin, that the sinning must stop if the one involved is to remain clear before God?" He firmly advises other pastors to follow his suggestions:

> What if those advocating acceptance of remarriage are wrong and Christ meant exactly what He said when He called remarriage adultery? O Lord, just help us! Think first, of all we have told that remarriage was all right, and they are lost. Then think of our own souls as we stand before the judgment bar of God and hear God pronounce an awful indictment against us for going our own way. We may have a retort now but we will be speechless then! O Lord, I would rather be safe than sorry, rather be safe than lost. God help us to see the danger of our deliberations and the consequences.

The author, a pastor, made no recommendations as to how he would have handled any children born of the remarried couple.

There are, however, more and more Christian counselors who are well qualified and sensitive. I believe many Christians would feel more at home with them than with non-Christian counselors, where they may need to defend the importance of prayer in their lives or their belief in putting Christ first in their priorities.

There have also been extremes where dedicated, sincere Christians have become so embedded in the world of psychology that they have lost some of the excitement and joy of their Christian faith. "Psychology and Christianity have never been real good friends," explains Gary R. Collins ("How to Tell Which Way to Go," (*Eternity,* January 1975). He points out:

> Two men were effective in at least making the first steps towards a truce: Paul Tournier and Norman Vincent Peale. Originally, Tournier wrote for doctors, trying to convince them that, in addition to his physical nature, man has a psychological and spiritual dimension. In his own medical practice, in fact, Tournier had seen how the power of Christ could change lives. Tournier now has an enthusiastic following around the world and has written books on a wide range of topics: marriage, growing old, loneliness, fear, child rearing, guilt, suffering, sin and repentance, to name a few.

Peale is best known for *The Power of Positive Thinking,* in which he makes frequent references to the Bible, but, in Gary Collins' opinion, his message comes through with a greater emphasis on enthusiasm and helping oneself. Conservative Christians look on both Peale and Tournier with a bit of suspicion. In most evangelical minds, Clyde M. Narramore stands out as the first psychologist to take the Bible seriously. He has helped to convince many Christians that psychology has something to offer.

In recent years, writers such as Keith Miller, Bruce Larson, and John Powell have gained quite a following among Christians. Miller states in the introduction to his book, *The Becomers:* "Instead of a doctrinaire and vertical exclusiveness with God, the new Christian is moving toward deeper and more honest personal relationships with people in the world—as well as with God."

One objection to extremely conservative Christian psychologists is that they base all their therapy on the patient's accepting Christ (on their terms) and are unable to help a patient who would not so accept Christ. On the other hand, Christians might object that secular psychologists, no matter how well-trained, are leaving out the most important thing in the patient's life (faith in Christ) and trying to work around that "dependent" relationship to help the patient.

John Broger, a Christian counseling authority, has admonished the church to take the lead in counseling. Disturbed that secular psychiatrists are now counseling church members, he points to the historical ability of Christians to deal with their own problems with God's help. He believes that church-centered, biblical counseling can assist people in developing life-styles based on God's truth.

The American Psychiatric Association, in their

newsletter, "Psychiatry-at-Work," reports that a panel of ministers and psychiatrists met to discuss ways in which a special knowledge of each could be helpful in the other's work. Individual ministers of all denominations are obtaining special education so they can help persons in their congregation with marital problems. They are aware that understanding modern psychology can be very helpful and they are eager to apply the principles of human behavior to their congregation.

When a couple approaches their pastor for marital counseling and he believes they need more in-depth therapy than he is qualified to give, it is encouraging to them if their pastor is well-informed and able to recommend places where they may obtain help. It is also helpful to a professional counselor to know that a couple's pastor is supportive of psychiatric work.

Couples sometimes hesitate to let their pastor know that their marriage is not perfect and that they could use some advice. But ideally, they'll turn first to their pastor for help. In fact, when a couple asks their pastor to perform their marriage ceremony, he may offer to see them a few times to discuss stress they may be experiencing. This is especially beneficial for second-timers, because they face complex problems. Many times their own pastor may be best able to work with them and they will need no additional help. Their pastor can also be a tremendous support to them when they find new or recurring problems discouraging.

My pastor, Ken Stangeland, had been especially supportive to me and my family during the years I was divorced, so we've always known that he would be very willing and available whenever we need his help. At first I hesitated to let him know that Marv and I had a few problems. I thought that, since he had listened to me for so many years, he would think, "Oh, no, not her again." But he has since assured me he isn't thinking that. Since he is trained as a professional counselor, we've found his help to be doubly meaningful.

When Marv and I asked Pastor Stangeland to marry us, he invited us to take the Taylor-Johnson Temperament Analysis Profiles. We each answered pages of questions on how we perceived ourselves and each other. Pastor Stangeland filled out a graph to demonstrate our results. Then we discussed with him the implications for our marriage. The nine categories on the test were: nervous vs. composed; depressive vs. lighthearted; active social vs. quiet; expressive, responsive vs. inhibited; sympathetic vs. indifferent; subjective vs. objective; dominant vs. submissive; hostile vs. tolerant; and self-disciplined vs. impulsive.

Marv and I found ourselves at opposite ends of the scale in one category. Marv went over the top in being methodical and a perfectionist; I went way down to the bottom because of my tendencies to be impulsive, changeable, and free-wheeling. Pastor Stangeland pointed out that often couples with opposite traits end up blending well. He also said that most individuals see the other person very differently from how that person sees himself. We learned much about ourselves and each other from the tests and the conversations.

Marv and I also happened onto another source of counseling. After we'd been married a few months, I began to experience periods of dizziness and light-headedness. This was especially frightening since I drove 52 miles round-trip to work each day. I was also frequently irritable over minor issues. I couldn't understand what was happening to me. I had been in good health, and I was under far less stress than while I was raising three children by myself.

My friend Sandy Tymoszenko, a professional counselor, recommended that we make an appointment with a physician at the Wholistic Health Center nearby. With this unique concept of total health care, a physician works hand in hand with a counselor to minister to the whole person—body, mind, and spirit.

After a physical examination, the doctor asked if I was under emotional stress. I said I didn't believe so, since I had recently remarried and felt more content than I had been for many years. He commented that often newly married second-timers face more problems and make more major decisions than they realize. Consequently they experience emotional turmoil they aren't even aware of.

He explained that a staff pastoral counselor was available if I wanted to work with him. I didn't believe my dizziness was connected with our adjustment problems, but I agreed to talk with Pastor Jim Gaynor. The very next week Marv injured his ankle and we decided that as long as he also needed to come in for treatment, we would see Pastor Gaynor together. The session went well, and we agreed to continue. We discussed everything from problems encountered in being a stepparent to the various anxieties I was experiencing in trying to be a good wife.

Later I discovered physical reasons for my dizziness (I was diagnosed as having hypoglycemia), but Marv and I benefited greatly from the counseling.

Again I would like to stress—if you are seeking counseling, be cautious and shop around. If necessary, play detective and do some investigating. Information about the person or agency you are considering should be available. As Dr. Brun said, "Remember, *you* are the consumer." Keep searching till you find a skilled and sensitive person with whom you feel comfortable.

Another important consideration is whether to approach counseling as a couple, whether each or one of you should embark on individual counseling, or whether family therapy would be best.

Sandy Tymoszenko warns against parents sending their child off to a counselor alone, implying that the child is at fault. She believes that it is not usually the child alone who needs attention, but the entire family. There are times, of course, when a child might need individual therapy, but this must be handled with a sensitive understanding of the child's needs.

Pastor Stangeland often brings in the whole family so he can observe how they interact. Sometimes, depending on how the family groups up, he may work with some sub-system. He might ask a father to come in with his three children. If he recognizes that one person within the family needs individual attention, he will recommend this. By this time, the individual has become acquainted with the counselor and the process and should not feel threatened if seen alone.

If you enter a counseling program, ask for an estimated projection of how long counseling should continue and when the counselor expects that progress will be visible. This will give you some criteria to measure against. I recommend evaluating the counseling by asking, "Is it working?" A pastor may be an objective person to discuss results with.

After a reasonable period of time, if nothing has changed, discuss this with your counselor. Be open with your feelings. There are no set rules, but it is a waste of time and money to continue if problems loom as large as ever. Remember that you are free to seek help elsewhere.

On the other hand, how great it is to run into a couple who announces that they, along with the counselor, have decided they no longer need regular counseling, but have made quarterly appointments to stop in for a "marriage checkup."

CHAPTER SIX

Instant Parenthood

Even though Marv had coached Tim's Little League team since before our marriage and we participated in many outings and sports activities with the boys, they remained emotionally detached from Marv. This was frustrating to both of us, but especially discouraging to Marv. We prayed about it.

We had been married nine months when Marv sprained his ankle. Ligaments and tendons all up his leg were damaged, and he was in much pain. He spent most of the winter on crutches.

Suddenly the boys saw Marv in a new light. His size had in some ways overwhelmed them, and they always thought of him as big and strong. But when Marv was on crutches and in obvious pain, he didn't seem as threatening or overwhelming.

The first week after Marv's accident, I returned home each evening to find both boys in bed with him, surrounded by games and books. They played Battleship and Checkers and did their homework with his help. This was the first real camaraderie between them and Marv. My first thought when I saw them was from Corinthians: "My grace is sufficient for you, for my power is made perfect in weakness." Marv learned, as did Paul, that "when I am weak, then am I strong." In his weakness he now made great strides with the boys; eventually, we could even thank God for Marv's injury because of the good that came of it.

Marv's experience reminded me of an especially meaningful chat I had with Timmy. I, too, had been in a horizontal position when it took place. It was a beautiful spring Sunday, about a year before I met Marv. The kids and I went biking and stopped to rest in a small neighborhood park. I sprawled out in the grass, gazing up through new green leaves to the beautiful sky. Timmy came over and sprawled out on the grass next to me. And he started talking . . . about his school and friends and many other things. I realized then that my getting down to his eye-level had a lot to do with his talkativeness.

Parents rarely recognize the awesome impression their size makes on children. Youngsters sometimes feel threatened by tall or big people. They connect size and authority, so they may become frightened or angry at adults who tower over them, simply because they feel powerless next to them.

When Marv scolded him, Danny had retorted, "You think you're so big." Marv didn't mean to use his strength as a threat, but to the boys it seemed like Marv used his size against them, especially when he spanked them. Marv couldn't believe the boys could actually fear or be angry at him because he was big. Then one day it dawned on me that it would be hard for Marv to understand how it felt to be threatened by someone so much larger. By the time Marv was the same age as our boys, he was almost as tall as his mother. His father had died and his mother didn't remarry until Marv was 16. So Marv, at the ages of Tim and Dan, didn't experience fear of a large parent. He therefore had trouble understanding this fear in his stepsons.

Dr. Jim Shakelford, who is well over six feet tall, told of a similar experience. He was trying to communicate with one small boy in a hospital where he worked. Nothing much was happening until he realized how awesome he appeared to this little child. When he found a way to communicate eye to eye, conversation improved considerably.

We knew another reason the boys seemed to need to keep Marv at arm's length was their loyalty to their natural father, whom they visited one or two weekends a month. They believed they would be disloyal to their natural father if they established a meaningful relationship with Marv. Sometimes they'd forget and become involved in something with Marv, but then they seemed to catch themselves and retreat again. Every time they found themselves slipping into this new relationship, they felt guilty toward their natural dad. They couldn't seem to understand that Marv was not attempting to replace their own father, but wanted to be another person who cared about them.

Their natural father seemed afraid, too, at first, that Marv would take the boys' love away from him, even though Marv told him he had no intention of trying to do this. His attitude became less tense when he remarried and became a stepfather himself. The boys now have a fairly relaxed situation; they have a nice stepmother who is kind to them and a great stepdad who brings many new areas of interest into their lives.

Once both their natural parents remarried, the boys became more accepting of the situation. Until then, they hoped their father and I would remarry and they tried to manipulate situations in an attempt to bring us together. Now that we're both remarried, they've accepted their two sets of parents quite matter-of-factly. Danny was once told by his teacher to draw a picture of his family. Without hesitation, he divided the paper in half and drew a picture of one set of parents on one side and the other set on the other side.

But this acceptance of the situation did not come easily for anyone—Marv, the boys, their natural father, or me. I often found myself in the middle. I could see Marv's determination and his disappointment when things didn't turn out as he hoped. But I could also recognize the uncertainty of my small sons and I empathized with them as well.

I knew I should be more patient in many situations. For example, I found it difficult not to pull rank from time to time. I would say, "But they have always reacted like that" or "They will get over this phase; they got through the others." This would remind Marv that I had been their parent a lot longer and he would then feel he had no choice but to retreat. I had, in fact, been a parent for 16 years before I met Marv, and since Marv had no children from his first marriage, I honestly believed his expectations of children's behavior was often idealistic.

Timmy came up with his own unique reaction to Marv's disciplinary measures. When he is especially frustrated, he ducks into the bathroom and locks the door. Then, to let out his momentary anger, he presses his thumb emphatically on the release lever of the hot lather dispenser he gave Marv for Christmas. As the lather oozes out, Tim's anger cools off. We've tried to explain to Tim that this is an expensive way of handling his anger, but he doesn't seem convinced.

Marv is willing to admit after two years that he did in fact come on a bit too strong. In his eagerness to assume the role of a parent, he had rushed in head-on. This often frustrated the kids—and me as well. He has slowed down considerably now and lets many things go by that once would have bothered him.

When we first were married, I was very willing to back off and let Marv take charge whenever he wanted. But when I began to believe he was coming on too strong, I would defend the kids. The result, of course, was a divided front. The kids wasted no time in their efforts to widen that small crack in the wall and were very eager to get us into a disagreement over discipline. Now I realize how important it is that we work together as a team and I try harder now to back him up.

"Those who find themselves 'living with other people's children' often face overwhelming obstacles" claims Brenda Maddox, author of *Half Parents: Living with Other People's Children*. Maddox estimates that about one million children acquire stepparents each year, following death or divorce, full-time or on a weekend basis.

She continues, "The stepfamily is open and tough. It is not a bad place to live, for those who can accept the uncomfortable fact that many of the tensions between stepparents and stepchildren will be inevitable as long as spouses are replaceable and parents are not."

The care and discipline of stepchildren has caused the greatest stress and distress among remarried couples with children, according to our own interviews as well as our library research. Like many other problems discussed, the problems couples experienced with stepchildren usually came as a surprise. Each couple had been prepared to make certain adjustments, but they rarely had any idea of the tremendous stress the children would put on their relationship.

Invariably, couples with very young children told us how much easier it is for couples with older children because older children would better understand the situation. Couples with older children said they wished the children had been younger and more pliable when they married.

Young stepchildren may need an especially caring individual to meet their needs. They may expect more than the new stepparent is able to give. Older children, accustomed to a certain style of family life, may be thrown into an entirely different setting with new rules and boundaries. They naturally prefer the familiar—even if it was inferior to the new setting. If the children are in the adolescent stage, their typical rebelliousness will probably be exaggerated because of the added complications of being a stepchild.

Stepparents are often disappointed when their stepchildren do not display the gratitude they believe they have coming. Natural parents don't seem to give this as much thought—they raise children expecting them to make demands on their parents. If the natural parent makes a special effort to comment on the new stepparent's attempts to relate to the children, this encouragement can go a long way.

Florence Pauls, a stepmother and educator, urges all stepparents to

> be kind to those children. You may not be able to love them the way you would your own, although sometimes you can, but they are so vulnerable. They haven't learned yet even how to handle the problems of just living. They have a right as children to be treated with great gentleness, but also firmness. If you don't believe you can behave in this way, you just don't have any right to become one of their parents. When you marry that guy or gal, you marry that person's children, too—you really do. You'd better think it through before you take it on.

At what point does a stepparent actually become a "parent"—if ever? The instant a child is born, its natural parents become "parents" whether they live up to the responsibility of that title or not. But when a couple remarries and one or both have children, the point at which the spouse becomes a stepparent is not cut and dried. Legally, you could argue that a person becomes a stepparent at the time wedding vows are exchanged. But most couples we interviewed indicated that the point when the stepparenthood relationship became meaningful both for the adult and child rarely coincided with the couple's wedding day.

The fear in a child's eyes is not to be underestimated by optimistic adults. A child may be frightened by the new arrangements, even though the fear is unfounded. Sandra Tymozenko, who counsels adolescents and adults, describes a child's emotional turmoil when one or both parents remarry:

> It is important to emphasize that children who are coming in as stepchildren have suffered a loss. This is so important for the parents to recognize. Anyone experiencing a loss must go through a cycle of emotions which need to be worked out. Talks should be had with the children regarding the loss of their parent, either through death or divorce. Even if the natural parent is alive, their absence from the home is an obvious and painful void to the child. They should be given an opportunity to express their feelings. And it is never acceptable for the new stepparent to come in and announce, "Look, here are the new rules—abide by them."

My children each perceived Marv's arrival differently. Pam, at age 16, liked Marv very much. Her only problems with him usually involved his strictness and what she called his "old-fashioned viewpoints." Both Marv and I insisted on an earlier curfew than she would have preferred. Yet she accepted him as a parent even before we were married, introducing Marv and me to new friends as "my parents."

One other response from Pam did not show up immediately. It was less a reaction to her new stepparent than hesitance to relinquish a role she had assumed after I was divorced.

Pam took on a great deal of responsibility for her younger brothers while in high school. She even missed some after-school activities to baby-sit. When Marv arrived on the scene, Pam liked him and was happy to see me remarry, but she also felt less needed at home. She had a vague feeling that "now that Mom has Marv, she doesn't need me anymore." We didn't perceive this at first, because she seemed happy with the new freedom our marriage gave her. But gradually we came to realize how much Pam had been parenting her brothers. She found it difficult to relinquish that role.

We reassured her that I had appreciated very much her willingness to take on so much responsibility, and that, even though Marv was now willing to take some of this responsibility off her shoulders, we would always remember and be grateful for the support she gave when I needed it. We encouraged her to take advantage of her new freedom and participate in some activities she had missed out on earlier.

It worked out as we had hoped. Soon after starting classes at George Williams College, Pam won a tennis tournament. She also became a cheerleader while managing to keep up her grades. Soon we were financially able to have some necessary orthodontic work started on her teeth. So her life has done quite an about-face since Marv and I married.

At the same time, I believe Pam gained more than she lost in having to assume responsibility during our difficult times. She has learned much about the complicated role of parenting. She recognizes my mistake in marrying young and its long-range implications. She is planning a career working with juvenile delinquents and I believe her interest in helping others stemmed from her experiences. And Pam and I will always share special memories of those years I was divorced. We used a lot of elbow grease moving into four different homes and hitching up our camping trailer on weekend trips.

Pam's faith in God was strengthened, too. Along with her brothers and me, she experienced firsthand how God cares and provides for his children.

Once some neighbors called on us, inviting us to visit their nearby church. While we realized they had a fine ministry, I was serving as youth director of our congregation and Pam was in confirmation class. We felt very much a part of our own congregation.

Our visitors became persistent. They ended up making some derogatory remarks about our church, and they told me pointedly that their conservative denomination would be better for my kids. At that point Pam rushed to my defense. They asked her to prove to them that she was a Christian. I suppose they wanted to hear the Four Spiritual Laws by memory or something similar, but Pam went one better. She simply told them, very matter-of-factly, how we had experienced God's presence in our lives and guidance in our decisions. She told them of answered prayers. And our visitors went home. I doubt that they were convinced, but they knew when to quit.

Pam found a second opportunity to give testimony to her faith in a college sociology course. Her instructor was evidently hoping to make the point that a person's environment has a determining effect on the person's entire life. Pam wrote a rebuttal paper based on our experiences. She described how, with God's help, our own determination, and support from our friends, we were able to overcome many limitations and setbacks. I am grateful to the Lord that Pam came out of these years of responsibility with such a positive outlook.

When Jack and Marilyn Cushman married, they saw similar reactions in her sons. For two years the boys had assumed the role of "man of the house" and had helped discipline the two younger children. Marilyn and Jack discussed before marriage the discipline of Marilyn's children. They agreed that Jack would "lie low" for six months or so, until they had established a fairly comfortable relationship.

Marilyn was brought up with loving parents who were quite lenient. Jack, on the other hand, was brought up by loving but strict parents and tends to follow their example. Also, he had been on the police force. In court with juvenile offenders he often heard the judge blame parents for not setting proper rules for their children. He is, therefore, an avid believer in kids obeying rules.

Jack and Marilyn, although they sometimes disagree, usually work out a middle ground. And, while Marilyn's older sons were not enthused about her remarrying, after four years they are now happy with the situation. They respect Jack and occasionally seek his advice.

If parents live with their stepchildren while their own children live with the other parent, the children living in another home may worry that their parent will begin to care more for the stepchildren and forget all about them. Sadly, this sometimes happens.

Ray and Joy Strutz have tried to be both sensitive and fair in their relationships with Ray's two sons, who visit weekends, and Joy's two sons, who live with them. They discovered that her boys were better able to accept Ray's discipline after they could see for themselves that Ray treated his own sons, of similar ages, the same way he treated them.

Ray was hesitant to correct his stepsons at first, because he didn't want to set back their relationship and because he wasn't sure if his wife would agree with him. It took a few years before he felt at ease correcting them immediately, without first discussing the situation with Joy.

Ray and Joy stress their belief that you can never talk things over with your children too much. They make a point of telling the kids what is going on. Ray believes that most stepchildren experience turmoil and need a lot of companionship. He and Joy spend much time with all four of their boys. When they head out on a vacation, all the kids are included. They now have a baby of their own, and the four older boys all enjoy him.

Joy wants to be a friend to Ray's sons and tries to avoid excessive discipline. At first, she says, "One boy would pick on the other and I would hope they'd quit before I'd have to step in and say something. I will raise my voice to them occasionally now, but I can still yell at mine a lot easier."

Just about the time I was finishing this book, I was invited to speak at a writer's conference in Abilene, Texas. At the luncheon table, I was seated next to Marianne Kwiecinski, a writer who had won a number of awards at the banquet the evening before. I complimented her and we started to "talk shop."

Then she changed the topic of conversation and took me by surprise when she asked, "How does your husband like his new stepchildren?" I laughed and explained that he likes them, all right, but that all of us had had to make big adjustments. Then she softly announced, "I know just what you mean. I have nine stepchildren, which my husband has custody of."

"Wow!" I said. Nine stepchildren—and she looked so young. As it turned out, she was quite young. She has been married seven years to Chet, a man 20 years older than she, and she believes they have a very good marriage. They have one son from their marriage, Ben, and she described her husband as being very devoted to him, as he is to his other children.

"How did you handle all this?" I asked. She answered at length:

Well, I always wanted a big family. I was an only child and my desires for a large family were reinforced after I saw *The Sound of Music*. Actually, I saw that movie four times. And I saw other movies and read books that were similar, such as *Cheaper by the Dozen* and *Yours, Mine and Ours*.

I thought I was realistic, and I knew it wouldn't be all that romantic, having a large family. But I was sure it would be fun.

Well, I discovered that, while the problems are amusing to read about when they happen to others, and even amusing to look back at when they've happened to you, while they're happening, it's not fun!

When I first got married, I was really idealistic. I thought I'd make a few rules, such as "No eating the front room," and then I expected everything to run smoothly. However, I had a daily encounter with the "mysterious person."

"Who left the mayonnaise out?" I'd ask. "Who ate the hamburger I'd planned to use for the casserole tonight?" "Who bounced the ball against the wall on Saturday morning at 7:00?" "Who stuffed orange peelings under the couch?"

No one ever knew. The mysterious person had me stumped. You can't discipline the mysterious person if you can't find him. This was one of many problems I wasn't able to solve.

I had organized everything so well. Chores would be rotated weekly. There would be no doubt what was to be done and who was to do what. But it was very difficult to check up on and administer these rules.

Eventually, I developed the attitude, Oh, well, it is only a matter of time until they grow up. Time did help.

There were a number of good things I had going for me. Joan and Mary, our two oldest girls, were old hands at delegating authority. I relied on their ability to give orders to the younger children. That way I didn't feel like such a Simon Legree.

Mary was special in another way, also. She had the gift of noticing little things and showing appreciation for them. "The kitchen looks nice—you washed the floor," she would exclaim. That gave me a warm feeling because someone had noticed. Then it didn't seem quite so bad when 10 minutes later the shiny surface seemed to self-destruct. I discovered that so many kids could mess things up pretty fast.

It was the little things, though, that usually got me down, but then again, it was the little nice things that got me through. Chet was especially loving and supportive. Whenever he would see that I was really tired and discouraged, he would make a cup of tea for me and give it to me with a hug.

I asked Marianne if she wanted to comment on marrying someone quite a bit older than herself. "Well," she laughed, "Chet is very active and full of energy. When I can't keep up with him, he teases me and says, 'I'm just going to have to trade you in for a younger model.'"

Due to this age difference, some of Marianne's stepchildren are not much younger than she. At the time of their marriage, Marianne was 24 and Chet was 45. His oldest child at home was 19, and the youngest only 7. She became more of a friend than a parent to the older kids. She appreciates their acceptance of her, and she says they didn't appear to have any hesitancy or objections because of her age.

While in Abilene, I had an opportunity to appear on a local television talk show to discuss my book on divorce. Afterwards, the talk show host, Michael Henry Martin, shared his own experiences in his second marriage. After telling me how especially understanding and considerate his new wife, Carol, is, he described the following situation.

Shortly before his first wife remarried, Michael stopped by to chat with the man she was planning to marry. Since this man would soon become stepfather to his son Lance and Lance would be living with him, Michael asked that he please be good to Lance. His ex-wife's future husband was very understanding and reassured Michael that he would treat Lance kindly and considerately. And he did—until the tragic day he was killed in an accident, shortly before his own son, Jason, was born.

Michael continued to pick up Lance for regular visits, and he rapidly became acquainted with his son's new young stepbrother, Jason. Michael began to include Jason in occasional outings, even though he was a baby. By the time Jason was a year old, he was almost always going with Michael and Lance. When Michael remarried he had already been, in his words, a "two-son daddy" for four years. Carol is completely accepting of this relationship, which Michael appreciates.

Which all goes to show that, when we become involved in step-relationships, we can never predict the long-range consequences—and we'd better be prepared for adjustments. But step-relationships also bring unexpected blessings.

Loni Whitfield has two sons who live with their natural father and spend one weekend a month with her and her second husband and their little daughter, Cherie. Loni explains that, while she certainly wishes circumstances would have allowed her sons to live with her full-time, she can see that God is using her boys to witness to their father, stepmother, and stepbrother. Because of her sons, their stepbrother, Kirk, already believes in Jesus.

She told how one day her pastor found a note on his pulpit from her son John. It read: "Please pray for my father and stepmother, as they do not know Jesus."

Loni added, "The fact that my second husband and I are both Christians would have to be the most important aspect of our marriage. This adds a powerful dimension to it, along with our human desire to make it work this time."

We wouldn't want to leave this very serious subject without a few reminders that, in addition to all of its responsibilities, stepparenthood does have its humorous side.

Shortly after Marv and I were married, our Danny was telling someone about our family, and he said, "Now we have a new stepfather and an antique car." We weren't sure which made the greater impression on Dan—Marv or his 1928 Oakland.

When John and Sharon Burner went to his class reunion just a few months after their marriage, they won the award for being the most recent newlyweds. They also went on to win the very next award for having the most children of anyone there. (They have a combined total of six.) Only second-timers could enjoy such a distinction.

CHAPTER SEVEN

Remarriage after Death of a Spouse

Maria von Trapp (of *Sound of Music* fame) had been married to Baron von Trapp only a few months when she began to worry about whether she would be able to make him as happy as his first wife had. In her autobiography, *Maria,* she describes her feelings:

> The second marriage when the first marriage was not happy must be a great thing. You can do all the things your poor husband has been deprived of, and you can really glory in being bigger and better every day of your life. However, if the first marriage has been a very happy one, then it is not that easy.

One day after Maria had been married a few months she asked, "Georg, how can I make you happiest?"

He looked at her and said, "By being exactly like Agatha" (his first wife).

Maria says:

I wanted to surprise him. So, fortified with pencils and pad, I made the rounds of those cousins who had been her best friends and near to her same age. I went from one castle to another and finally ended up in Vienna, where her sister was living, all the while filling my notebook with the answers to my stereotype question, "What was Agatha like?"

"Well—she was very quiet. Very kind. She loved to knit. She did not like to hike or other sports. She loved having babies, and so was always either expecting one or nursing one." That was the main outcome of my research.

I was blown up with good intentions. While I was pretty much convinced that Agatha and I were like night and day and it would be hard to find two women who were more opposite, there was no question in my mind that I could bridge the gap and simply *become like Agatha.* Even as other people want to learn as grownups to play an instrument and therefore dedicate hours and hours to practicing on the cello, the violin or the piano, I devoted my time to my project: to become like Agatha.

First I bought knitting needles and wool, went back to Nonnberg, and found a nun who could show me how to knit. Sadly enough, I had never learned. Having decided to knit socks for my new husband, I found myself a comfortable easy chair in which to sit from then on and to act like Agatha.

I must have knitted about five inches worth of stocking when Georg came into my room, stared at me, and said, "What are you doing there?"

Meekly I answered, "I am knitting, Georg, like Agatha." He shook his head and said, "Let's go bicycling."

That disturbed my program.

"But, Georg," I said, "Agatha did not go bicycling with you. Please sit down with me and let's talk."

He shook his head, got himself a chair, sat down and looked me over. He couldn't quite understand what was going on. I stared at my knitting because every time I glanced away, I dropped a stitch and frowningly had to regain it.

I was waiting. I had heard that Georg used to sit with Agatha by the hour and tell her stories from the navy. Why didn't he start?

Georg still looked unbelievingly at my handiwork and said laughingly, "When do you think those stockings will be finished?"

Now I was hurt. Of course I didn't knit very fast yet. In fact, I could hardly knit at all. But he didn't see my goodwill.

So I stubbornly kept on knitting and knitting and waiting and sitting in my chair for Georg to see my great love, because wasn't I slowly becoming exactly like Agatha?

This lasted about ten days. Then Georg came into my room again, got his chair very close to mine until our knees touched, put his hands on mine so I couldn't continue knitting, and said, "Now tell me, what is bothering you? We're not going for hikes anymore. We're not playing volleyball, we're not making music together, not bicycling anymore—WHY?"

By then tears came streaming down my cheeks and I cried aloud, "Because I want to become like Agatha!"

Georg took my knitting and threw it in the corner. He pulled me out of my chair and held me tight, and said, "I didn't mean it that way. If you are as kind as she, that is good enough for me. Otherwise, please be yourself."

And that was the end of that. From that moment on I was really in love. The real me—Maria —with my Georg.

Maria learned that the best solution to her dilemma was to simply be herself. Many other second spouses have to learn that same lesson.

The concern Maria experienced is quite common, especially if the mate's first spouse died. Most people have trouble remembering anything unpleasant about a deceased mate. (See chart, page 122.) They tend in fact, to exaggerate that person's good points. Obviously, this can put a second spouse in the uncomfortable position of being successor to a saint. Sometimes the effects are devastating. Awareness of this tendency to idealize a dead mate can help the new spouse to take it in stride.

Maria might have put paper and pencil to better use by listing her own qualities that attracted her husband. If you know what attracted your spouse to you in the first place, you can try to continue to be attractive to him in the same way. Developing a new skill or taking on a new hobby can also help build a strong self-image, giving one an appealing sense of self-confidence. Second-timers benefit from concentrating on the future rather than the past.

Ann Bedford lost her first husband in a car accident. She is now the wife of a Methodist minister, who is divorced. Rev. Bedford dated five or six women before he met Ann. In Theos Newsletter he says, "When I met Ann, she was a radiant, happy, self-sufficient person who happened to be a widow." What a beautiful description. Wouldn't Ann be making a mistake if she became so concerned over whether she was pleasing her new husband that she stopped being radiant and happy and became tense and anxious?

I almost made that mistake. I worried so about whether I was making Marv happy and whether he was enjoying our family that I became frustrated whenever he said anything slightly critical or negative. When I realized what I was doing, I became even more tense. I imagined that Marv was sorry he had married me and I read this thought into his most casual comments. Then, because fear often expresses itself through anger, I'd lash out defensively and say things I'd be sorry for later. I've now overcome many feelings of insecurity, and our marriage is better for it.

Persons in a second marriage who were happily married the first time have some advantages. Experience may have taught them the benefits of being willing to give a little, to communicate honestly, and to commit oneself to marriage. Having experienced a meaningful marriage, they are likely to seek out new mates with similar goals and continue their pattern of success.

But sometimes persons whose marriage had been good will be so lonely after their spouse dies, longing for the security and happiness their relationship provided, that they jump into a second marriage.

121

PATTERNS OF ADJUSTMENT
FOR WIDOWED AND DIVORCED PERSONS

DIVORCED PERSONS

1. Ego loss. Damaged self concept.

2. Frantic rush for new companionship to restore ego loss.

3. Some sexual experimentation to restore ego loss.

4. Rejection of former spouse.

5. Anger and resentment against actions of former spouse.

6. Terrible loneliness learning to live alone if you did not receive custody of children.

7. Presence of other partner in visitation forces review of difficult past.

8. Pattern of use of children as pawns in angry disputes with former mate or as information source (spies).

9. Children's feelings are not always considered in the action because parents' emotions are overwhelming.

WIDOWED PERSONS

1. No ego loss. Ego support.

2. Little desire for new companionship because of grief.

3. Awful sense of separation, but little sexual experimentation.

4. Memory focus on loved one, usually pleasant.

5. Bitterness over injustice of the death or toward loved one (he did not care for himself).

6. Loneliness is dimmed by presence of children and much support from others.

7. Glorification of the past and a treasuring of memories.

8. Children are seen now as more important and valued because they help continue the family structure.

9. Needs of children and their feelings are usually valued and often paramount because they offer security.

10. Children have deep reaction of guilt, rejection, and anger.

10. Children feel grief, loneliness, and resentment over exit of deceased person.

11. The continued battle between former partners can be constant and hard on the nerves.

11. No fencing between partners because only one partner is living.

12. Divorced face constant pressure for financial support since the settlement often falls short of need.

12. Widow does not have as critical a financial pressure because money is often inherited.

13. Strong need for love and affection. Frequent rejection or avoidance of divorced by friends and family intensify this need.

13. Need for love and affection not as intense because of happy memories, much support from family and friends.

14. Divorced feel they have an edge over widowed in competition for new partner. Date more often.

14. Widowed view divorced persons as competitor for available partners. They date less often.

15. Confusion over who should be future spouse and where and how failure occurred in first marriage.

15. Recollection of happy events in marriage. Blotting out of negative aspects of marriage relationship.

16. Desire for early remarriage. Short engagements.

16. Desire to remarry not as intense. Far fewer widows ever remarry.

This chart was prepared by Dr. Kenneth D. Barringer, a counseling and consulting psychologist who has a practice in Iowa. He formerly wrote a monthly column, "The Single Parent," for *The Christian Home.*

Because they are eager to recapture happiness, they may marry the first available person who comes along, closing their eyes to serious potential problems within the relationship.

Then there are those whose marriages weren't fantastic, but who liked the state of being married. They liked doing things with a mate, even if their marriage had many rough spots. They too may tend to jump into a new marriage too soon.

Most persons who have lost a spouse through death agree that it is essential to give oneself adequate time to work through the grief cycle before considering remarriage. The bereaved pass through various phases of grief, and only then are they emotionally ready to enter into a new relationship.

Unfortunately, some widowed people believe that "no one can ever take his (or her) place." They pass up opportunities to build new relationships, and find themselves traveling a lonely road.

Statistics inform us that there are almost twice as many widowed persons as there are divorced persons. Almost three million U.S. families are headed by widowed individuals. Of the widowed, 10 out of 12 are women.

When Bea Decker was widowed with three daughters 16 years ago, she made up her mind to turn her grief into constructive channels. She began an organization called THEOS (an acronym for They Help Each Other Spiritually and also the ancient Greek word for God). THEOS is a nonprofit foundation (11609 Frankstown Road, Pittsburgh, Pa. 15235) with chapters throughout the United States. Its purposes include helping the newly widowed work their way through grief and helping those who have been widowed longer cope with day-to-day problems of being alone. They address not only emotional and social problems, but also such practical matters as finances, home care, automobile care, and raising children alone.

A natural reaction after a spouse dies is to experience feelings of guilt over things said or unsaid and dreams left unfulfilled. Probably every widowed person has these feelings to some degree, no matter how happy their marriage was. Especially traumatic, however, are the feelings of guilt suffered by survivors who had some responsibility for their spouse's death. Perhaps they were driving the car in which their spouse was killed, or maybe they failed to recognize how emotionally disturbed their spouse was until it was too late. But God is able to heal these hurts, too, and here our Christian faith is especially meaningful.

I remember well the intense feelings of guilt one man endured for a long time after his wife took her own life. For years she had asked her husband to attend church with her, but he showed little interest. Ironically, after her suicide, it was church members who ministered to him and brought him to Christ. He became a dedicated Christian and in the years to come brought many people to the Lord himself.

But for a long time, his guilt feelings were almost unbearable. Here he was, actively involved in the church, just as his wife would have liked. Why couldn't he have shared this joyful experience with her when she lived? He could acknowledge God's forgiveness but had trouble forgiving himself.

God worked in him and slowly healed his inner pain. Eventually, he decided to ask God to find him a new wife. God led him to a dedicated Christian widow. Today they are married and working together enthusiastically in their church. Many lives have been touched by their ministry.

CHAPTER EIGHT

Humoring Your Spouse

"That's not funny!" I snapped.

"Aw, c'mon, don't you have a sense of humor?" Marv teased.

That *really* made me angry. "Of course I do! What an unfair thing to say! Why, I have a great sense of humor!" I assured him in no uncertain terms.

Marv didn't look convinced. "Why am I getting so worked up about such a little comment?" I wondered, and quickly answered my own question. "Because I don't happen to see anything funny about this situation, that's why!"

Later, when my emotions were back in neutral, I tried to explain to Marv that, although he might not realize it, I did have a perfectly good sense of humor. However, I felt his joke was at my expense. I pointed out other times when I'd felt the same way.

Marv felt I was being oversensitive. "I didn't mean

127

anything by it," he insisted. "Can't I even kid with my wife?"

Eventually (much, much later) we realized the entire incident had been a combination of quite a few things, and we agreed that we needed to learn to take ourselves less seriously and to laugh more. Many of the best times we've shared were when we laughed together.

"Remember the Olivia Newton-John concert?" I asked Marv, and we both chuckled.

My friend Jan and I had decided to surprise our guys by getting tickets for an Olivia Newton-John concert. We were so speedy about getting to the box office that, to our delight, we were offered first row seats.

The night of the concert, we decided to dress up—the guys wore suits and Jan and I had new outfits. When we arrived at the International Amphitheatre, we noticed that we were considerably more dressed up than the people around us.

We worked our way through the crowd to where the concert was being held. To our surprise, we found ourselves facing what appeared to be a corral. We assumed this was for the livestock exposition also scheduled at the Amphitheatre. We found our way down to our first row seats.

"I sure wouldn't want to be sitting here in the first row if we were watching a rodeo instead of listening to a concert," Marv stated emphatically.

"That's for sure," we all agreed. "We'd get our laps full of dirt—and probably a lot of other stuff as well."

We noticed one other dressed-up couple sitting

near us, looking equally confused. We decided Olivia must have some sort of mobile stage that could be elevated and set down in the middle of the field.

Then they let in the bulls. We stared in shock as we realized we *were* attending a rodeo. But what happened to Olivia?

About an hour later she appeared . . . far, far off on a stage at the opposite end of the corral. She was the intermission entertainment. And she was suffering from a sore throat and cold, so we had to strain to hear her.

By this time we began to see how silly this whole incident was. Once we started laughing, we could hardly stop . . . until the folks around us (who came to see a rodeo) started glaring. "Obviously, they don't have much of a sense of humor!" we decided.

Every time we think of that night, we laugh and recall how much fun it was, after all.

Without a doubt, marriage provides ample opportunities to put humor to good use and also provides the necessary motivation to cultivate and improve one's sense of humor.

Humor can be an effective tension reliever in stressful situations if appropriately applied. When we learn to laugh (or at least chuckle softly) at how seriously we are taking ourselves, we relieve not only the outward tension but also the inner emotional tension of everyone involved.

We may be tempted, however, to use humor as a coverup for wisecracking or sarcasm. How often have we heard someone put down their spouse and then attempt to justify their words by saying, "I was just kidding, of course." This is not to imply that every time anyone kids around they have an unconscious (or conscious) desire to criticize. Sometimes we are honestly "just kidding." Very often, too, people who feel unsure of themselves make a feeble attempt to say something funny or clever, but the comment ends up sounding like a "put-down."

When we're in the grip of uncontrolled emotion, our thinking can be absurd and completely inaccurate. Difficult as it is, making a determined effort to step back and look at the situation as objectively as possible can sometimes snap us out of it and give us the benefit of recognizing the humor in the predicament. Usually it is difficult to see humor in a tense situation until quite some time has passed. However, making a point of attempting to look at events from a humorous perspective can at least provide the time necessary to regain self-control.

Even when we have legitimate reasons for anger or frustration, humor can sometimes ease the situation enough to prevent words being said that can never be retracted.

There is also a danger in laughing off serious statements, thereby giving the impression that what someone said isn't important enough to take seriously. This can frustrate a spouse who feels deeply about something and whose mate looks on it as a laughing matter. Most of us have discovered also that it is much easier to laugh off someone else's viewpoints or opinions than to laugh off our own feelings.

People who have a lively and imaginative sense of humor are especially appealing. They are fun to be with and seem to bring with them an atmosphere of optimism and joy in living. While it comes quite easily for some people to see the humor in everyday situations, most of us have to work at cultivating our sense of humor. But it is undoubtedly worth the effort—so I have been told!

It is also easy for us to blame others for the lack of joy and humor in our lives. We've heard people say, "If you lived with my spouse, you wouldn't laugh either." But with Christ's power we can rise above the temperaments of those around us. Sure, a pessimistic person can rob us of joy—but only if we let them.

In his book, *Are You Fun to Live With?* Lionel Whiston makes this thought-provoking statement:

> To react to others is to let them control us and determine our moods and courses of action. To be committed to Christ and filled with his love is to let the Master chart our desires and behavior as we respond to him. Difficult? Yes, but possible when we give ourselves to let him do in and through us what we cannot do ourselves.

More often than not, it is the occasional discouraging situation, when our stress level is low, that may blow out of proportion and cause tempers to flare. It helps a lot if at least one of the two is able to maintain composure and see the humor in the situation. A perfect example is this experience shared by Mrs. Jean Platt in *Sunday Digest:*

When my husband left for work that morning, the day was sunny and bright, and I was jubilant! Spring had finally arrived and I was eager to tackle some long-postponed household chores. Gradually, however, my mood changed as blue skies grayed over and a steady drizzle began. The garage man called to say that our car needed major repairs, my cake for the P.T.A. bake sale turned out to be something less than a gourmet item, and my ancient washing machine refused to wash. Events continued in this dismal vein, and by 6:00 P.M. I was ready to chew the head off the first person who came along.

At 6:15 P.M. my husband became that unfortunate person and, when he opened the kitchen door, I gave him a verbal barrage that rattled his eardrums. I told him what was wrong with our household—the neighborhood—the city—the country—indeed, the whole wide world. And I blamed him for most of the local grievances.

Throughout the long, horrendous diatribe, my husband never relaxed his grip on the doorknob and, when I finally paused for breath, he quickly backed outside and closed the door.

In a moment, he flung it open again and, entering for the second time, smiled pleasantly as he inquired, "Well, other than that, how did your day go?"

A reusable private joke can also be a successful tension-reliever. Just a word or sentence that has a backlog of humor and sentiment can do wonders for jangled nerves.

John and Joyce Basiger shared how a very real concern early in their marriage later became their reusable joke. When they were first married, John worried that this marriage, like his first, wouldn't last. He tried to warn Joyce about his tendency to continually find himself in some sort of minor disaster. Evidently he felt she didn't take his warning seriously enough. Now, whenever something of this sort happens (like the time they were in downtown Chicago and each thought the other one had brought money . . .), he reminds her, "I warned you, but you didn't believe me." And often Joyce kiddingly retorts, "Well, you warned me, all right, but I didn't believe it could be this bad."

John believes the situation which most needs to be handled with humor is the first time a second wife meets a first wife.

While interviewing couples, Marv and I had fun with the question, What is the funniest thing that has happened to you as a couple?

Their answers were very revealing. A few couples took their efforts to "make this marriage work" so seriously that they didn't seem to have time for fun.

A bit of ingenious humor solved what could have been a touchy problem for one newlywed couple. Returning from their honeymoon, they broached the subject of whose bed they should sleep in. She had an antique bedroom set that had been in her family for years. He had an ornate brass bed that he felt he absolutely must have in his new home. For quite some time they went round and round, trying to solve the dilemma. Then they came up with an answer.

They have her bedroom set in their bedroom—and his bed is the focal point of their unique living room. In a comfortable corner, it is decorated with huge pillows lining the walls. Guests can leisurely lounge there. It is more comfortable than an ordinary couch and conducive to informal conversation. What could have caused a rift in their relationship was handled with a combination of humor and creativity.

The subject of beds came up in another way in our interviews. Often a person entering a second marriage is adamant about not sleeping in the same bed the new spouse slept in with his or her first spouse. I once happily benefited from such a situation. I inherited a good bedroom set when a friend of mine remarried. Her new spouse-to-be was so enthusiastic about her getting rid of the bed that he gallantly delivered it to my door.

Unfortunately, humor can also be a weapon. Some people use sarcasm or wisecracking to put down their spouse in the company of others. They laugh at them, not with them. This is a sign of serious problems in the marriage. Such people need to find more therapeutic and mature ways to vent hostility.

One last story about a bed. One night Marv and I were lying in ours, discussing the events of the day. I had been waiting for an opportunity to tell him about something that mildly upset me.

"Marv," I began, "lately, every evening at the dinner table, as soon as you gobble down your food, you get up, put your dirty dishes in the sink, and disappear with an 'I've got to go do something.' Then you leave me at the table (with or without the kids) while you hurry off to do some project. Now it isn't that I don't appreciate your ambition. It's just that I prefer to leisurely eat our evening meal and talk together. When we were dating, we used to talk for hours on the phone. Now, we are always too busy doing something else. It seems lately we hardly ever have time to just talk to each other. Do you understand what I mean?" I concluded, almost pleadingly.

"Yes, I guess so," Marv replied hurriedly. Then he sat up, got out of bed, and said, "I've got to go do something." And he left the room.

I was stunned. Evidently he hadn't understood a word I was saying. I turned my head to the pillow and tried to decide whether to laugh or cry in frustration. Then the phone rang.

I reached over to the bedstand and picked up the receiver, wondering who was calling this late.

"Well, hello there," a masculine voice replied. "I thought I'd give you a call so we could have a nice long talk." It was Marv, calling on Pam's line.

I burst out laughing. In a humorous way, he was letting me know he heard and understood my frustration. It was a perfect example of humoring one's spouse.

CHAPTER NINE

The Church and Remarriage

Shortly after my first husband and I separated, I found a job in a Christian publishing house, which I felt would be meaningful as well as challenging. When I applied for the position, I explained that my husband was living in Wisconsin and that we had separated. At that time, though, I said I did not intend to get a divorce, since I still hoped that in the days and weeks ahead we would be able to work things out and be reconciled.

However, after what seemed a very long year and a half, during which time my husband and I received, together and separately, professional and pastoral counseling, things had not improved at all. After a great deal of agonizing, I decided to get a divorce.

I felt I should explain to my employer my new status as a divorced woman. I was concerned about how he would react, since most of the executives and many of my coworkers were very conservative in their Christian viewpoint on this subject and I wasn't sure how I would be accepted in this new role.

I went to my immediate supervisor, who had been a minister before entering the religious publishing field. He was quite understanding about my divorce, mainly because he felt I was more or less the "innocent party." (This view, while it certainly made my position much easier, at the same time made me feel uncomfortable and hypocritical, since I do not believe there is ever really an innocent party in a marital breakup. One person may be more to blame than the other, but usually both contribute to the conflict.)

My boss offered to speak to the head of the company for me, but he said he did not believe that he or anyone else would be uncomfortable about my working there now that I was divorced.

However, he added, "It might be a different story if you were getting remarried. We probably would not approve of that."

Since remarriage was the furthest thing from my mind at that time, I was not disconcerted by his statement. However, it remained indelibly imprinted on my mind and later came back to haunt me.

I was familiar with scripture references to divorce and remarriage. I had read and reread these passages many times and had done much soul-searching and praying before deciding to get divorced.

Eventually, I concluded divorce was the most logical solution to my problems, for reasons I explain in detail in *The Hurt and Healing of Divorce*. But for many years the words of Jesus in Matthew 19 kept me from seriously considering this alternative. Those words seemed to indicate clearly that divorce was not the right decision for us. I asked myself over and over, "What *is* right? Is it right for my children and me to stay in a situation that is destructive and unstable? Does God really want my children to spend their formative years, when they are so impressionable and vulnerable, in this setting?"

Finally I realized that, for me, the key to my dilemma was my understanding of God and his Word. As I studied my church's catechism, the words "We should so fear and love God" had been deeply imbedded in my heart and mind. I knew well that we shouldn't underplay obedience to God.

But then I also asked myself, "Why did God give us his commandments to live by? Was it because he was rigid and demanding?" I decided it was because he knew best the guidelines that would give us the greatest overall peace and happiness and make our lives most meaningful. Therefore, his laws indicate that perfect will of God with which we should all try to comply.

However, the New Testament has an equally clear message regarding God's grace and love and forgiveness. My question was, "Would God's love and forgiveness allow for divorce and possibly, in the future, remarriage?"

To the question of divorce, I decided yes. The question of remarriage I tabled until a later time.

Shortly after I was divorced, I was worshiping in my church one Sunday morning when I felt a surge of joy bubbling up within me. We were at the point in our liturgy when we confess our sins and receive assurance of God's forgiveness. I was overflowing with love for God, who had forgiven my sins and given me a new start.

I realized that, during the last few years, before I made the decision to divorce my husband, I was beginning to feel resentful toward God. I felt trapped in an intolerable situation, yet I was desperately afraid God would not forgive me if I worked my way out of it. I feared that God would desert me if I divorced my husband, and I couldn't bear the idea of living without God's guidance.

Now I knew that, not only did God not desert me, he graciously forgave me and filled me with his love and joy. In the years that followed, he continued to guide me and provide me with many wonderful answers to prayer, as well as surrounding me with loving Christians to support and help me.

In fact, I believe one of his beautiful answers to prayer was to provide me with my new husband.

One spring weekend, my children and I were camping at the Bible camp affiliated with my church. As I sat around the large community campfire with my children, I was very much aware that I was the only single parent. All around me were couples of various ages, some sharing a blanket, some with youngsters on their laps. Watching fathers fishing with their children and seeing couples playing tennis had also made me aware of my single status. But sitting by the campfire, I felt especially alone and lonely.

Later I sat down with my prayer notebook and wrote out a request: "Dear Lord, it would be so nice to have someone to love and to share things with. If it is within your will, please send a man into our lives, to become part of our family. And Lord, please send someone who:

1. is a Christian

2. would be willing to join our church, which is so meaningful to me and the kids

3. loves children

4. likes camping

5. is an avid reader

I prayed about this long into the night. My prayers reflected my selfish interests and needs. How marvelous that God understands us so well and tolerates our selfishness on occasion.

When we returned from that camping weekend, we had to vacate the house we were renting. Finding owners who would rent to a divorced mother with three children was no easy task, so most of my prayers were concentrated on asking the Lord's guidance in finding a new home for our family. And God did answer that prayer.

However, from time to time during the house-search, my prayers also included a request for a new husband. And my prayer partner, Florence, prayed with me one morning about a husband, a house, and after-school care for my children the coming fall. All in all, though, I felt that I was asking a lot from the Lord and was hesitant to ask for too much too soon.

Less than two months after we moved into our new home, I was introduced to Marv. By that time I was so busy with settling into our new home and keeping up to date on my job that I had almost forgotten about asking God to send a Christian man into my life. But obviously God hadn't forgotten.

A few months after meeting Marv I ran across the prayer I had written while on the camping trip. With a mixture of surprise and excitement, I read through the specific requests I had made of God regarding a new husband. Marv "checked out" with every specific request I had made—he had recently become a Christian, he had attended a church of my denomination as a child and now was already attending my church, and he liked my kids, camping, and reading. I could hardly believe my eyes. Every request on my prayer list fit Marv to a tee.

I would never use this as an argument that God allows remarriage—there would be far too many loopholes for skeptics. But I would like to outline here a few theological explanations which I believe allow for divorce and remarriage.

Of course, I do not believe divorce should ever be taken lightly or become an "easy out." Also, remarriage involves many complications to carefully consider. However, I believe it is more often the church, rather than the Scriptures, which, in zealous legalism, sentences the divorced Christian to lifelong punishment. Congregations willing and even eager to welcome the ex-convict and former drug addict

141

into their midst treat divorced persons almost as lepers, with a stigma intended not only to shame but to permanently scar.

The church sometimes creates special complications for persons planning to marry a previously married person, even though they, themselves, have never been married. Joyce Basiger said she wished the church hadn't made it so difficult for her to marry John. Their church had been very hesitant because John had been married before, and this somewhat dampened their wedding plans.

I received a letter from a woman who read *The Hurt and Healing of Divorce*. She and her husband had both been previously married and divorced. They joined a church discussion group which they found especially meaningful — until the group discovered that they each had been divorced. With much pain and disillusionment, she and her husband decided to leave the congregation because of the prejudice displayed against them, even though they believed in the church doctrines.

Another disturbing experience was that of a husband and wife who both felt God's call to become missionaries in Africa. They made arrangements to sell their business and put their beloved house up for sale. However, the request put in to the foreign mission board of their denomination was refused—because she had been divorced 22 years earlier. The denomination would not forget or forgive.

Though they were disappointed and stunned, they approached God with this problem and he worked things out in his own way.

Pastors often find themselves in the midst of this controversy. Many are not sure how to resolve the stand of their denomination with the dilemmas faced by many couples considering divorce or remarriage. Pastors have seen situations in which divorce was obviously the lesser of two evils. They may also have seen second marriages between two sincere Christians that were obviously healthy, satisfying, and providing a good environment for the children. How, then, can a pastor remain true to the church's stand on divorce and remarriage if this stand appears inconsistent with Christ's demonstration of love and forgiveness—as to the woman taken in adultery (John 8:3-11)?

A pastor who becomes divorced faces this dilemma personally. When Rev. Marcus Gravdal, now of Barrington, Illinois, decided after 18 years to end his unhappy marriage, he was pastor of a 7000-member congregation and he had a daily radio program and a weekly television broadcast. He immediately resigned as pastor and withdrew from the clergy. Since he, himself, had previously believed divorced pastors were somehow less than they ought to be, he felt it would be wrong to stay on.

Gravdal moved to Illinois and became a businessman. He also became involved in ministry to an inner-city black congregation. After he remarried, Gravdal and his twice-widowed wife became active lay members in a church in Barrington. When the pastor serving this congregation submitted his resignation, Gravdal's name was brought before the calling committee and he was delighted when they asked him to become their pastor. His request for reinstatement into the ministry was granted. Both Gravdal and his wife appreciate God's grace and guidance in their lives.

In 1973, Rev. Charles Arthur Trentham, a leading Southern Baptist clergyman, separated from his wife after 30 years of marriage and she went to Reno for a divorce. He remained at his church for 11 months, then married a divorcee who was a soloist in his choir. Although most Southern Baptist churches would not have called a pastor who was divorced and remarried, First Baptist Church of Washington, D.C. offered him its pulpit. When President Carter and his family moved to Washington, they selected this church for worship.

What do the Scriptures say about divorce and remarriage? The words of Jesus in Matthew 5:31-32, Matthew 19:3-9, Mark 10:2-12, and Luke 16:18 cause most concern to Christians. Paul also refers to the subject in 1 Corinthians 7:10-11.

I believe that these passages must never be picked up and taken as an entity, out of context. They must be looked at in the light of the entire New Testament message.

We know that New Testament believers were set free from the severity of the Mosaic law. For example, no longer are we commanded to stone to death those guilty of adultery. In John 8, Jesus demonstrates compassion and forgiveness to the woman taken in adultery.

Why, then, did Jesus speak out so specifically and harshly on the subject of divorce and remarriage?

These statements seem to put Christians in the uncomfortable situation of offering to other believers full pardon of all sin and failure, while at the same time insisting that marital failure be forever penalized. Isn't this incongruous with Christ's treatment of people here on earth?

Jesus often spoke out of Mosaic law. Apparently the Old Covenant period lasted until Christ's death and resurrection and the sending of the Holy Spirit.

Dwight Hervey Small, author of *The Right to Remarry,* has delved into scriptural teachings on divorce and remarriage. Says Small, "To understand the Kingdom is to understand His ethic. An ethical transition is clearly present in the ministry of Jesus, which looked back to the Mosaic Law, yet forward to the eschatological Kingdom."

These words of Jesus are nowhere repeated in the Epistles, although Paul alludes to them in his First Letter to the Corinthians. However, Paul's teachings differ from those of Jesus. Paul was writing to the Corinthians in answer to their specific questions— not necessarily in answer to our specific questions today. Again, taking this passage out of context and isolating it can lead to misinterpretation.

The Corinthians were struggling with the question of which is better—marriage or the single life. They believed Jesus would be returning within their lifetime, which colored many of their actions and thoughts. We must also consider this passage in light of the "present distress" that Paul refers to. Evidently there was considerable turmoil and the beginnings of persecution of Christians. Paul was very practical and believed the church's outreach would best be served if Christians would concentrate on Christ. He may have said, "It is well for them to remain single, as I do," so believers wouldn't be tempted to put family interests before the church.

In this context, we read Paul's words: "To the married I give charge, not I but the Lord, that the wife should not separate from her husband (but if she does, let her remain single or else be reconciled to her husband)—and that the husband should not divorce his wife" (1 Cor. 7:10-11).

Paul did not include Jesus' words, "except for unchastity," possibly because he was not going into specifics but refreshing their minds as to God's basic intentions for marriage. This should also be our aim.

Divorce was commonplace in Paul's time. He may have been reminding the Corinthians, as Jesus had done, that divorce is by no means something to take lightly or to rush into. Paul then says, "but if . . . ." He was realistic enough to recognize that the ideal is not always possible.

Jesus did permit divorce on the grounds of unchastity (which in this context is usually understood to mean many acts of adultery). Since Paul did not discuss "unchastity," it seems the Corinthians were not asking about that but rather were concerned about Christians married to non-Christians. Small says:

> It would appear Paul is addressing himself to the general question of whether a Christian should divorce a pagan partner because that partner is a pagan. The answer clearly is *no*. But there is the more urgent matter of the pagan

spouse who wants out of the marriage. Paul says that in such instances the Christian is not to fight it, not to try everything possible to keep the marriage together. Paul is a bit more realistic than many pastors in this regard. He elevates personal peace above the retention of the mere formality of marriage. He recognizes the internal death of marriage as a very real possibility, and especially the nonexistence of a spiritual marriage as certainly a detriment to the Christian spouse, especially if the unbeliever wants out. Paul doesn't try to argue that this is an impossible situation on the biblical grounds of "one flesh," any more than he intimates that the Christian spouse will be an adulteress or adulterer if she or he remarries. . . . Nor does he intimate that the Christian partner should remain unmarried in the hope that the non-Christian mate may at some future time become a Christian and want to return to the marriage.

Now let's get back to the words spoken by Jesus. In Matthew 19:1-9 we read:

Now when Jesus had finished these sayings, he went away from Galilee and entered the region of Judea beyond the Jordan; and large crowds followed him, and he healed them there. And Pharisees came up to him and tested him by asking, "Is it lawful to divorce one's wife for any cause?" He answered, "Have you not read that he who made them from the beginning made them male and female, and said, 'For this reason a man shall leave his father and mother and be joined to his wife, and the two shall become one flesh'? So they are no longer two but one flesh. What therefore God has joined together, let not man put asunder." They said to him, "Why then

147

did Moses command one to give a certificate of divorce, and to put her away?" He said to them, "For your hardness of heart, Moses allowed you to divorce your wives, but from the beginning it was not so. And I say to you: whoever divorces his wife, except for unchastity, and marries another, commits adultery."

Note to whom Jesus was speaking: the Pharisees, whose express purpose was to trick Jesus into saying things that would alienate him from the people. Since the people were divided on the subject of divorce, here was an ideal controversy for them to use to try to manipulate Jesus into a corner.

Jesus anticipated their trickery. He knew that whether he sided with Hillel, who said a man might divorce his wife for any offense or for dislike of her, or with Shammai, who maintained that divorce was unlawful except in the case of adultery, he would be putting himself directly in the midst of the controversy.

Jesus was not afraid to stand up for justice. But he chose, rather than take sides, to call attention to the perfect will of God regarding marriage—that is, that a man would have one wife.

Jesus was not skirting the issue, but rather confronting it head on. By going back to Mosaic law, he bypassed the teachings of Hillel and Shammai. He admitted that Moses did allow divorce. But it is believed that Moses was in fact trying to discourage divorce. Moses was facing a defensive people among whom divorce was widespread. By telling them to write a bill of divorcement, perhaps he hoped to force them to stop and think before rushing emotionally into divorce. Taking time to put complaints in writing might serve as a "cooling-off" period and some couples might be reconciled as a result.

Jesus was also uplifting the position of women. He considered them too valuable to be dismissed lightly. He was also protecting them. Many women were divorced by selfish spouses for trivial reasons. They had little way of earning a living, and many divorced women became prostitutes.

The words of Jesus in Matthew 5:31-32 read: "It was also said, 'Whoever divorces his wife, let him give her a certificate of divorce.' But I say to you that every one who divorces his wife, except on the ground of unchastity, makes her an adulteress; and whoever marries a divorced woman commits adultery."

These words are from the Sermon on the Mount, the whole of which contains, as Small says, "the highest ethical mandate to come from the lips of Jesus."

> Look at the simple declarations and direct commandments from the Sermon; is this not legalism for the most part? Is this not ethical perfectionism quite beyond all present human capability and expectation? Is this not, indeed, every bit as much an obedience-ethic as the Mosaic Law —only greatly intensified? Nothing is said here about man's inability to perfectly obey, nothing about the Holy Spirit as the needed Enabler. There is no reference whatever to the new relationship which belongs to those who are the

New Creation in Christ. It is purely a righteousness attained by right inward attitudes and outward obedience. It is law, not gospel.

Jesus seems to be reinterpreting the Mosaic law at
a higher level. He adds, "For I tell you, unless your
righteousness exceeds that of the scribes and Pharisees, you will never enter the kingdom of heaven."

Jesus' words in the Sermon on the Mount, including his declarations on divorce and remarriage, con-
tradict or at least contrast with 1 John 1:9: "If we
confess our sins, he is faithful and just, and will forgive our sins and cleanse us from all unrighteous-
ness."

I believe it was because Jesus was teaching his fol-
lowers about God's pure, perfect righteousness and
will that he was so strict. Small says that Jesus was
making it abundantly clear that "God never lowers
the level of divine righteousness to its human accom-
modations." This high level would certainly include
God's high standards and divine intentions for
marriage.

Included in the Sermon on the Mount are six
examples of the superior righteousness of the kingdom which the Messiah shall establish. How many
Christians do you know who are consistently able to
follow these rules? "If someone slaps you on the
right cheek, turn and offer him your left. If a man
wants to sue you for your shirt, let him have your
coat as well" (Matt. 5:39-40 NEB). The Sermon, on
the other hand, does not include discussion of redemptive solutions that God provides for Christian

failures. It talks not at all of God's forgiving and renewing grace that is offered to us in the Epistles.

If ever we are clearly told that marriage is part of God's plan and that God does not approve of divorce, it is in these passages.

In remarriage, then, we commit a sin—according to Jesus' words, the sin of adultery. How shall we handle that sin, now that we have fallen short of God's perfect will? Is this sin unforgivable? Are we excommunicated from God and the church? Obviously not, since Jesus himself demonstrated compassion and forgiveness for adulterers. The greater sin, I believe, would be to enter carelessly into marital bonds, assuming our escape clause via Jesus' forgiveness.

I accept divorce and remarriage as sin in God's eyes, when mirrored by his perfect will. We have fallen short of the ideal and have failed to attain God's best intentions for us.

I am deeply grateful that Jesus made very obvious his acts of forgiveness as he dealt with the people around him. He offered "living water" to the woman at the well who had had five husbands and was living with still another man. He offered forgiveness of sins to the woman (thought to be a prostitute) who washed his feet with her hair. We see proof of his willingness to forgive sexual sins. Jesus saw beneath the exterior to our deepest needs and our sincere intentions.

That is not to say that I believe the sin of adultery was not very serious to Jesus. It was so important that he said it would be better to cripple oneself than to be tempted to lust and commit adultery.

Author Pat O'Brien told that she interviewed numerous couples in her research for a book on what makes successful marriages work. She found not one happily married couple who subscribe to the *Open Marriage* sexual freedom. She did, on the other hand, learn of couples whose marriages were destroyed by attempting to live with such a liberal, free attitude. She found that it had not brought the peace and excitement that its proponents claimed, but rather disillusionment and depression.

Jesus also discussed internal aspects of adultery. He talked about the secrets of the heart and movements of the eye. A vivid example of the long-range pain that can eventually result from a simple "roving eye" is the sad story of King David, whose sins stemmed from lusting and acting on that lust. But David's story is also an example of how God forgives sinners who confess and change. David was a murderer and an adulterer, but he admitted his sins, and Nathan told him, "The Lord also has put away your sin; you shall not die."

Abraham was also an adulterer. He displeased God by impregnating his wife's maid. But after 13 years of silence in which God was chastening Abraham, God said, "I will not let you go," and he used Abraham to bless many people.

In both cases adultery brought much heartbreak. God forgave David and Abraham, but they lived with certain evidences of their sin.

Sometimes there is much pain within a second marriage. Repercussions from divorce may bring deep hurt to families. Guilt feelings, much like those experienced by King David before he received God's forgiveness, may leave deep emotional scars.

When we fall short of God's perfect will, we suffer because of the knowledge that we have disappointed God and because of the havoc sin causes in our lives and the lives of those around us. But what joy we find when, like Abraham and David, we experience God's freely given, forgiving love.

George MacDonald once said, "To love and to forgive are the luxury of the Christian. It is more than a duty, it is a high privilege."

But often churches forget to love and forgive. Individual Christians forget to love and forgive. They support hard and fast rules and allow for no exceptions. Some churches accept remarried, divorced persons as members but exclude them from church offices. Small asks:

> What Scriptural grounds have we, really, for discriminating against the remarried when it comes to service in the church? When Paul says that a pastor or elder is to be the husband of one wife (1 Timothy 3:2) he probably is referring to monogamy as opposed to the polygamy widely practiced in the heathen world. With this many ancient and modern authorities agree. It does not say, "married only once," but clearly "the husband of one wife." A remarried man fulfills this requirement beyond question!

A thought-provoking article titled "Is God Legalistic?" *(Presbyterian Journal,* Sept. 1, 1976), Eldon C. Stanton says:

> Now, in Christian love, I want to suggest that hard-and-fast rules without exceptions seem to limit God's sovereign grace. . . .
>
> Look at Abraham, for instance. . . . Abraham, the adulterer was still God's child. . . . Do you think God would allow such a sinner to become an officer in the Presbyterian Church?
>
> Perhaps King David is a more pertinent example. . . . Here was a murderer and an adulterer who became the apple of God's eye.
>
> Do you think God would allow such a sinner to become an officer in the Presbyterian Church?

How very reassuring, however, to know that many individuals and couples, even though rejected by a specific church or denomination, have kept their faith in Christ and even grown stronger in their faith in spite of this experience.

One such encouraging example is Dale E. Galloway. At age 31, his life was filled with the things he thought he wanted most in life. He was pastor of a large church in Oregon, which had grown tremendously under his pastorate. He had a wife and a son and daughter, all of whom he loved very much. He believed he had a happy marriage.

Then his wife announced that she did not love him and was divorcing him and taking their children 2500 miles away to her hometown.

He was beside himself with anguish, realizing that he had made mistakes and wanting so badly to make amends. But it was too late. He realized his role as a minister would be tremendously affected, as would every other aspect of his life. Never before had there been a divorce in his immediate family.

After crying out in frustration to God, he finally prayed, "God, my Father, I can't live without you. Forgive my rebellion. I place myself once again in your hands. Do with me whatever you want to do." And in that moment of yielding, commitment, and resignation to God, the Spirit of Christ came and ministered to him.

Slowly he began his journey from brokenness to wholeness. He discovered the universal principles for emotional and spiritual healing that God has provided, and by depending on God for his healing, he became stronger in his faith than ever before in his life.

To help others whose lives are broken, he wrote *Dream a New Dream*, describing his predicament within his church as follows:

> The fact I love God with all my heart and want more than anything else to be used in his service does not seem to matter. Any of the circumstances that brought the divorce about are not even considered. I am a divorced minister in the church I was brought up in, which brands me as a failure in the ministry. *To the officials of my denomination, I am a washout with no way to ever return to a position of pastoring one of their churches.* I understand there is nothing personal in this, that it is the blanket sentence passed on any minister whose home is broken by divorce.
>
> To most churches of a conservative persuasion, a divorced minister is a failure—period. Today my heart bleeds for the multitudes of men who have been washed out of their churches. Who, yes, have failed, but worse yet, have been brand-

ed failures forever. The church of Jesus Christ must be more redemptive than this.

Having been brought up in a conservative evangelical denomination, there was nothing in the world more of a failure to me than divorce. It was bad enough what others thought, but the failure I felt inside myself was like a 300-pound weight, being carried on my shoulders everywhere I went. A sense of failure can wipe a man out. From my own experience, I want to share with you how to define failure in a positive way so it will help you instead of hurt you.

In the following pages of his book, he states, "You were created for something greater to live with than a failure complex." His book is dedicated to helping people rebuild broken lives. He advises slamming the door on self-pity, applying healing medicine to emotional wounds, putting failure behind, and believing that the best is yet to come.

There is an exciting ending to his book. The Lord did still want to use him, much more so than ever before. Today, Dale Galloway is the founder and pastor of New Hope Community Church, Portland's first drive-in/walk-in church. His ministry reaches out to hundreds of people, many hurting in ways similar to his own.

And he has remarried. He describes his new relationship:

During this time, I felt all alone, whether I was with people or by myself. Hurting, hurting, I needed a good friend. It was a day never to forget when God brought into my life my best friend.

Her name was Margi. . . . Her father had been a pastor for many years. It has been our joy to communicate deep levels of feeling in ways which very few people ever have the privilege of sharing together. One of the greatest things we shared very early was our mutual desire to serve God with our lives. One thing I have never been able to get over was how Margi knew all about me in my brokenness, yet she loved me. To me, this is love. With each passing day, our friendship grew, and as it did, there was born a love that was to never die. . . .

The marriage Margi and I have together today is a tremendous success, because both of us are determined to make love our highest aim. It is this that fills our life with joy, with sharing, with enduring one another's shortcomings, with helping each other to overcome and become. My greatest delight is giving my love to my very best friend and wife, Margi.

It has only been a few years since his world tumbled in on him, but Dale has discovered that, because Jesus is alive and cares about us, no situation is hopeless.

Dale writes, "If I could give to a man only one thing, I would give him hope. The kind of hope the Psalmist wrote about when he said: 'For in thee, O Lord, do I hope' (Psalm 38:15). *A man who has hope can never be defeated.*"

Additional Resources

Dream a New Dream, by Dale E. Galloway, Tyndale House, Wheaton, Illinois, 1977.

The Half Parent: Living with Other People's Children, by Brenda Maddox, Evans, New York, 1975.

Hide or Seek, by James Dobson, Revell, Old Tappan, New Jersey, 1974.

Peoplemaking, by Virginia Satir, Science and Behavior Books, Inc., Palo Alto, California, 1972.

Remarriage, by Carmel Berman Reingold, Harper and Row, New York, New York, 1976.

Right to Remarry, by Dwight Hervey Small, Revell, Old Tappan, New Jersey, 1975.

Stepchild in the Family, by Anne W. Simon, The Odyssey Press, Indianapolis, Indiana, 1964.

Successful Stepparent, by Helen Thomason, Harper & Row, New York, New York, 1966.

DATE DUE

DEC 20 '85			
JAN 15 '88			
12.18.87			
8/24/88			

DEMCO 38-297